The Revelation of HEALING

Walking in the Power of Kingdom Healing & Deliverance

LARRY HENDERSON JR.

DOMINION
HBG

ISBN-13: 978-0692180990

ISBN-10: 0692180990

Published by Henderson Business Group (HBG), Intl.

Acknowledgments

To my King, Jesus Christ: I am amazed at Your infinite wisdom. I am amazed at Your patience and grace toward me. Thank You, for giving me the gift of revelation that I might do my part in this generation to bring about the restitution of all things.

To my beautiful wife: Tiffany, you are an amazing woman! Thank you for agreeing to stay with me on this Kingdom journey. All of your edits are priceless. Your prophetic vision is unwavering. Your beauty is ageless. Your smile is infectious. You are the lover of my soul and the keeper of my emotions. I Love You!

To my children: Thank you, Adonijah and Anaiah, for the hundreds of trips back and forth to the Church. Thank you for how you have graciously integrated the ministry and the never-ending visitors to our home into your lives. Your sacrifice is not lost on your Father. Your reward shall be great!

To my The Kingdom Advancement Center (KAC) Family: You are the greatest church in the world! Thank you for giving me the time and space necessary to write this book. Thank you for your undying commitment to live your lives according to the Word of God. Thank you for taking care of your apostle and pastor. May you forever be committed to "Teaching the Word, Perfecting the Saints, Advancing the Kingdom of God!"

Table of Contents

Introduction

The Body of Christ needs physical healing. I have witnessed too many Christians suffering without the healing for which Jesus died on the Cross of Calvary. Much has been said in the Church about healing. For the most part, it has been preached that healing was only meant to be the ministry of Jesus, His twelve apostles and the disciples of the early Church. Many believe that the gifts of the Holy Spirit, along with healing, died with the first century Church and the last apostle. Many sermons have been preached to defend this way of thinking.

I have personally wondered for years:

- Why do we not see many healings today?
- What is God's will concerning healing in the Church?
- Was healing just a means to lead people to Christ in the New Testament (NT) Gospels?
- Was healing just a secondary measure used by Christ to get His prospective followers saved? What is the purpose of healing in the Kingdom of God?
- Does God purposefully bring sickness and disease upon a person to teach them a larger spiritual lesson on humility or dependence on His power?
- Is sickness and disease a "Not my will but Your will be done, O Lord" discipleship training course?

There are so many questions to answer.

I have written this book to continue to foster a healing culture in the Church and to add logs to the ever-increasing flame of the restoration of the gifts of healings in our generation. It is necessary that we receive grace, and walk with God in our generation to release the anointing for healing in the Church today. It is not my goal to address every question about healing in this book, for there are already many great books on healing that we have been digesting for many generations. Instead, my goal is to write a concise volume about healing and deliverance and its relevance to the mission of the Kingdom of God, as Jesus instructed us to seek it first. Furthermore, this book aims to offer some practical exercises, aiding the born-again Believer with their walk in the gifts of healings and to apply it practically as we have witnessed Jesus and His disciples execute them by the power of the Holy Ghost within the Scriptures.

That said, I am not purporting to know everything about healing by writing this book. I will be the first to admit that I have experienced both success and failure while executing what I believe about healing. In fact, so did the early disciples of Jesus. This book, therefore, serves as another launching pad for the Body of Christ to remove itself from the classroom of healing and enter into the workforce, that we might exercise our senses and become skilled practitioners (disciples) of that which we have studied in the Scriptures.

There are many reasons why healing and deliverance is relevant, necessary and Scriptural for today's Church. The most glaring reason is that our King, Jesus Christ, purchased it with His own blood on Calvary's cross. Simply put, it is not a light thing to dismiss that which our Lord died to secure for the world and simply chalk it up as no longer needed or of major importance under the current dispensation of grace. We must fight harder to manifest that for which our King gave His life to secure. This is still the mandate of our generation, just as previous generations fought to manifest the gift of salvation, sanctification, full submersion in water baptism, the gift of tongues, and any other thing for which Jesus gave His life for the Church to receive in the Word of God. We have a responsibility, just as our spiritual forefathers, to press into the Kingdom to restore that which has been lost. Yes, there is much opposition to overcome in and outside of the Church to reclaim all of the manifestations of the Holy Ghost. This task is no less than what our Spiritual forefathers like Martin Luther sacrificed to restore the gift of salvation by grace through faith to the Church in his generation. Like Martin Luther, we must realize that our current Church leaders do not always have the right theology necessary to advance today's Church. No, we cannot turn back after we have come into the knowledge of the truth concerning any subject that has been revealed to us by the Father in heaven. Though, there are those that may persecute us for pressing forward in the Revelation of Healing we have received.

The Revelation of Healing

- Part 1 -
What is Healing?

The Revelation of Healing

- Chapter 1 -
The Revelation of Healing

Healing is a very sensitive subject in the Church today. The charismatic movement of some has caused many to become skeptical as to the real move of God concerning healing in the Church. It is easy to turn on your TV today and see so called "miracle workers and faith healers." We see them laying hands and blowing on those who claim to be sick. We watch with both skepticism and curiosity, pondering the authenticity of their claims. It seems the more we doubt, the more people seem to be healed. "Only believe," they say, "and you too can be healed."

Whether their claims of healing are real or not, the Bible is not afraid to speak about healing. In fact, healing was a major component of the ministry of Jesus Christ. He healed many that were sick, demon possessed and diseased. He commanded the man with the withered hand to *"stretch forth your hand"* and his hand was made whole. He commanded the sick of the palsy to *"Arise, take up thy bed, and go thy way,"* and immediately he arose and took up his bed. He laid hands on the eyes of the blind and they received their sight. He loosed the tongues of the dumb. He gave the deaf their hearing. He healed those possessed with demons.

Though healing was a major part of the ministry of Christ, many no longer see healing as essential to carry out the ministry of Christ in today's Church. Many see physical healing as a secondary issue as it relates to saving souls for Christ. They view it as an optional tool.

I must admit, I have struggled at times with the concept of healing. "Why do we not see many healings today as were manifested during the Bible days" is the obvious question? Why does it seem that God heals some and not others? Is God somehow selective? Is He somehow a respecter of persons when it comes to supernatural healing?

One of the most popular Scriptures in the Bible concerning healing is Isaiah 53:4-5. The multimillion dollar movie "The Passion of the Christ" begins with this Scripture. Anyone who knows anything about healing knows it:

Surely He hath borne our griefs, and carried our sorrows: yet we did esteem Him stricken, smitten of God, and afflicted. But He was wounded for our transgressions, He was bruised for our iniquities: the chastisement of our peace was upon Him; and with His stripes we are healed. (Isaiah 53:4-5)

This Scripture is obviously packed with a supernatural revelation about Jesus Christ. Obviously, through Jesus Christ we are healed of something; but what exactly? From what did Christ intend to heal us?

The answer to our anxieties and the solution to our situation is never far from us. Paul the apostle said it this way, "The Word is near you, it is in your mouth and in your heart, it is the word of faith, we are proclaiming" (Romans

10:8). In other words, the answer is in the text. Walk with me to Isaiah 53:4.

Surely

The word "surely" is a common Biblical word. It is a word used by Biblical writers meant to strike godly fear into the heart of the reader. Surely means "without doubt, no mistake, verily, truly, right at that moment or time, certainly, without question or explanation, most assuredly, a thing shall come to pass."

Whenever God instructs man concerning the eternal destination of his soul, He often uses the word "surely" in Scripture. For example, when God instructed Adam, He said, "*Of every tree of the garden, thou mayest freely eat: But of the tree of the knowledge of good and evil, thou shalt not eat of it: for in the day that thou eatest thereof, thou shalt SURELY die.*" *(Genesis 2:17, emphasis added)* When Jesus spoke to Nicodemus concerning salvation, He said, "*Verily, verily [or Surely, surely], I say unto thee, Except a man be born again, he cannot see the kingdom of God.*" *(John 3:3)*

"Surely" means that heaven and earth shall pass away before the thing that God has said will fail to come to pass. Surely means: be not deceived, God cannot be mocked, whatsoever a man sows, that shall he also reap. Surely comes with the force of heaven that ensures God's Word shall not return to Him void. Surely denotes that the Almighty God, Jehovah Elohim, means business and we'd better drop what we're doing and pay attention.

The Hebrew words for "borne" and "carry" are *nasa* and *cabal.* They both mean to lift, bear, take or carry away. They project the idea that one man would bare the load or burden of another by putting the load on his own back. If

15

two men were on a long journey and the weaker man could no longer carry his own load, the stronger man would *nasa* and *cabal* the other man's burden. He would place the load on himself and bare his brother's burden.

Isaiah is prophesying that when the Messiah would come, He would SURELY *nasa* or "bare" our griefs, He would SURELY *cabal* or "carry" our sorrows.

But what are our griefs and what are our sorrows?

The word "griefs" is the Hebrew word *choliy*. It is the Hebrew word for anxiety, calamity, sickness and disease. The word "sorrows" used here is the Hebrew word *makobah*. It means to have pain, anxieties or sorrows.

Simply put, this Scripture is saying that SURELY [without doubt] Christ has taken up our sicknesses and diseases. That SURELY [no mistake] Jesus has carried on His own back all of our sorrows and pains:

Surely [without doubt] He hath borne our griefs [sicknesses and diseases], and carried our sorrows [pains, anxieties, and sorrows]: yet we did esteem Him stricken, smitten of God, and afflicted. (Isaiah 53:4, emphasis added)

This interpretation of Isaiah 53:4 is eventually verified by Jesus Christ Himself during His earthly ministry in the Gospel of Matthew:

And when Jesus was come into Peter's house, He saw his wife's mother laid, and sick of a fever. And He touched her hand, and the fever left her; and she arose, and ministered unto them. When the even was come, they brought unto Him many that were possessed with devils: and cast out the spirits with His word, and healed all that were sick: (Matthew 8:14-16)

When I was a youth in the church, I used to hear my pastor preach many sermons about Jesus' work on the Cross. He would always preach that Jesus did not come to heal anyone of physical sicknesses, but rather of SIN sickness. The emphasis in these messages was that sin itself was an unruly enough evil in the world, that it was a deathly sickness all its own, and Jesus came only, truly to heal the world of the disease of sin, itself. I have found this to be a very interesting theological view in light of the point made here by Matthew the apostle. He gives an account of Jesus' ministry at Peter's mother-in-law's house when she was sick with a fever. The sickness, in this context, is obviously not a sin sickness but a physical infirmity. We know this because the author takes the time to tell us that *"He touched her hand, and the fever left her."* She was suffering from a physical sickness that probably would have killed her if Jesus had not made this house call. To further establish that we are not talking about simple sin sickness, we are also told in this Scripture that *"they brought unto Him,"* not SOME, but *"MANY that were possessed with devils."* These are not simply people with sin sicknesses but people that have been tormented by demonic beings called demons that are plaguing their lives. Jesus is recorded here as having a robust and definite solution: *"And cast out the spirits with His word, and healed ALL that were sick."* [emphasis added]

This leaves us with the question, "Why?" Why did Jesus heal ALL that were sick? The Bible gives us an emphatic and clear answer in the very next verse:

> *That it might be fulfilled which was spoken by Esaias the prophet, saying Himself took our infirmities, and bare our sicknesses. (Matthew 8:17)*

This is a direct reference to the Old Testament (OT) Scripture, Isaiah 53:4. Enough said.

Isaiah 53:4-5 reveals that Jesus ultimately died on the Cross for 4 main reasons:

1) To heal sickness and disease
2) To heal pains, anxieties and sorrows
3) To forgive our transgressions
4) To forgive our iniquities

Now it is time for the next logical questions. Why did Jesus give His life on the Cross of Calvary for these four things? Why is healing sickness and disease connected to the sacrifice of the Son of God? We will discover this in the next chapter as we uncover the law of sin and death!

- Chapter 2 -
The Need for Healing
(Uncovering the Law of Sin & Death)

I have been amazed by what the Scriptures say about healing! Believe it or not, the Scriptures speak quite substantially in both the OT and NT about God's will concerning healing.

Before we can understand the need for healing in the Bible, I must take you on a slight detour – a short story – to introduce you to the origin of sickness and disease. This leads us to discover, first, what the Scriptures say about the origin of sin in this world and the origin of mankind. Here is what the Scriptures say:

And God said, Let Us make man in Our image, after Our likeness: and let them have dominion over the fish of the sea, and over the fowl of the air, and over the cattle, and over all the earth, and over every creeping thing that creepeth upon the earth. So God created man in His own image, in the image of God created He him; male and female created He them. And God blessed them, and God said unto them, Be fruitful, and multiply, and replenish the earth, and subdue it: and have dominion over the fish of the sea, and over the fowl of the air, and over every living thing that moveth upon the earth. (Genesis 1:26-28)

And the LORD God took the man, and put him into the garden of Eden to dress it and to keep it. And the LORD God commanded the man, saying, Of every tree of the garden thou mayest freely eat: But of the tree of the knowledge of good and evil, thou shalt not eat of it: for in the day that thou eatest thereof thou shalt surely die. (Genesis 2:15-17)

And when the woman saw that the tree was good for food, and that it was pleasant to the eyes, and a tree to be desired to make one wise, she took of the fruit thereof, and did eat, and gave also unto her husband with her; and he did eat. And the eyes of them both were opened, and they knew that they were naked; and they sewed fig leaves together, and made themselves aprons. And they heard the voice of the LORD God walking in the garden in the cool of the day: and Adam and his wife hid themselves from the presence of the LORD God amongst the trees of the garden. (Genesis 3:6-8)

Here goes my short story. In the first chapter of the Bible, after God restores the world to an inhabitable form (Genesis 1:3-25), He makes man, Adam and his wife, Eve, in His own image and likeness. God's preeminent desire was for the physical realm of earth to function like the spiritual realm of heaven. Simply put, He wanted His Kingdom to come on earth as it is in heaven (Matthew 6:9). To accomplish this, He commissioned man to rule, to have dominion over all sea creatures, land creatures, and all the creatures of the air (Genesis 1:26-28). To complete His Kingdom coming plan, He put man in the Garden of Eden. The Garden of Eden was an earthly paradise where man had everything to fulfill the purpose of his existence. Its purpose was to provide an environment that looked and functioned like heaven on earth, so man could learn how to rule on earth as God rules in heaven, causing God's Kingdom to come. Voila! *"On earth as it is in heaven!"*

However, there is a catch (isn't there always?!) to God's Kingdom Coming Plan. To make sure man is able to exercise his ability to be "like" God, he must be positioned to truly choose the circumstances of his rule in the Kingdom. He must choose whether he wants to rule God's Kingdom way or some other way. Thus, God provides the Tree of the Knowledge of Good and Evil (Genesis 2:9). The instruction manual on this tree is simple: Man cannot eat of the Tree of the Knowledge of Good and Evil; the day he does, he will surely die (Genesis 2:17). Man is at liberty, however, to eat of any of the other almost infinite trees that will grow on the planet.

You know how the story ends... Man chooses to do the one thing he shouldn't do (don't we always?!) and sins by eating the fruit of the Tree of the Knowledge of Good and Evil. Thus, enacting the law of sin and death over all mankind. Here is the Biblical version:

> *Wherefore, as by one man sin entered into the world, and death by sin; and so death passed upon all men, for that all have sinned: (Romans 5:12)*

Hope you enjoyed my short story!

Uncovering the Law of Sin and Death

Now, what is the law of sin and death? Glad you asked! Simply put, sin produces death. Every person on this planet was born into sin (thanks to our super great grandparents, Adam and Eve); therefore, we were all born spiritually dead and will eventually die physically. The law of sin and death is more of a natural or spiritual law of physics than a civil, constitutional law. It is a law of cause and effect, of sowing and reaping.

However, Jesus Christ, the Lord, came to earth to undo the original sin of mankind:

For the wages of sin is death; but the gift of God is eternal life through Jesus Christ our Lord. (Romans 6:23)

For if by one man's offence death reigned by one; much more they which receive abundance of grace and of the gift of righteousness shall reign in life by One, Jesus Christ. (Romans 5:17)

That as sin hath reigned unto death, even so might grace reign through righteousness unto eternal life by Jesus Christ our Lord. (Romans 5:21)

There is therefore now no condemnation to them which are in Christ Jesus, who walk not after the flesh, but after the Spirit. For the law of the Spirit of life in Christ Jesus hath made me free from the law of sin and death. (Romans 8:1-2)

O death, where is thy sting? O grave, where is thy victory? The sting of death is sin; and the strength of sin is the law. But thanks be to God, which giveth us the victory through our Lord Jesus Christ. (1 Corinthians 15:55-57)

Jesus Christ, the Lord, returned to earth to undo the original sin of mankind. But, to do this, He had to overcome the power the law of sin and death held over mankind. He accomplished this by being the first man in the history of the earth to die without sin. Jesus' ministry that culminated on the Cross of Calvary was always meant to overturn the law of sin and death, and not sin ONLY, but also death. For this reason, Jesus not only concentrated on forgiving sins during His earthly ministry, but also healed the sick and raised the dead.

But why is physical healing necessary to overcome the law of sin and death?

Sickness and disease are both agents of death. All sicknesses and all diseases have one purpose: to bring us to death before our appointed time.

And as it is appointed unto men once to die, but after this the judgment: (Hebrews 9:27)

Sickness and disease are both agents of death. All sicknesses and all diseases have one purpose: to bring us to death before our appointed time.

It does not matter whether you have a common cold or colon cancer, every sickness and disease has the same goal: to bring a person to death. Some sicknesses work over the course of one's lifetime by weakening and wearying the body and the immune system year after year, like the common cold. Other diseases work more rapidly, especially if they go undetected, like aggressive forms of cancer. No matter the severity or magnitude, the goal is the same, to weaken the immune system for the end result of death. Even emotional and psychological diseases such as stress and anxiety have been proven by medical professionals to weaken the body and produce sickness and disease.

As the King of kings, Jesus had to wage war on sickness and disease (including pains, anxieties and sorrows) to completely defeat the law of sin and death. He carried sicknesses and diseases to the Cross to crucify these agents of death in open shame. This is why the Scriptures say:

Surely [without doubt] He hath borne our griefs [sicknesses and diseases], and carried our sorrows [pains, anxieties and sorrows] (Isaiah 53:4a, emphasis added)

The Kingdom Health Care Plan

What is healing? Healing represents the Health Care Plan of the Kingdom of God. Every Health Care Plan has a benefits package. The Health Care Plan of the Kingdom of God is no different. Its benefits were purchased by the blood sacrifice of Jesus Christ on the Cross. As mentioned in Chapter 1, there are four benefits to the Health Care Plan of the Kingdom of God as highlighted by Isaiah 53:4-5. These benefits can be broken down into two categories – the outer and inner man:

Outer Man Benefits:

1) To heal sickness and disease
2) To heal pains, anxieties and sorrows

Inner Man Benefits:

1) To forgive our transgressions
2) To forgive our iniquities

The Outer Man Benefits represent the benefits dedicated to healing the physical body, itself, including any emotional or psychological problems coming from the mind or soul. The Inner Man Benefits represent the benefits dedicated to forgiving the inner spiritual man, ultimately leading to salvation.

It is common in the Scriptures for the forgiveness of sins to be packaged with the healing of our bodies from sickness and disease. The Scriptures list the benefits of the Kingdom Healthcare Plan in several places. Here are a few Scriptures to consider:

> *Bless the Lord, O my soul: and all that is within me, bless His Holy Name. Bless the Lord, O my soul, and forget not* ***all His benefits:*** *Who* ***forgiveth all thine iniquities;*** *Who* ***healeth all thy diseases.*** *(Psalm 103:1-2, emphasis added)*

> *If My people, which all called by My Name, shall humble themselves, and pray, and seek My face, and turn from their wicked ways; then will I hear from heaven, and will* ***forgive their sin****, and will* ***heal their land.*** *(2 Chronicles 7:14, emphasis added)*

> *Is any sick among you? Let him call for the elders of the church; and let them pray over him, anointing him with oil in the Name of the Lord: And the prayer of faith shall* ***save the sick****, and the Lord shall raise him up;* ***and if he hath committed sins, they shall be forgiven him.*** *(James 5:14-15, emphasis added)*

I call this coupling of the forgiveness of sins and the healing of diseases in the Scriptures "The Package Deal."

The Same Sacrifice: The Package Deal

The basic concept of the "The Package Deal" is that Jesus died on Calvary's Cross for the healing of both our inner and outer man and did not intend for them to ever be separated. Our King spilled His blood one time so that the world, especially the Body of Christ, would have access to total healing. Jesus, therefore, did not intend for His Church to begin focusing on one over the other. This is ultimately why we do not see Jesus doing this in His earthly ministry. He did not intend for His earthly ministry to be analyzed by future generations of Bible readers as a dispensational anomaly, but as a continuous example to establish His Kingdom on earth.

If you decide to accept this (hermeneutical) view of the Scriptures, meaning, you are picking up what I am putting down, then, you must realize that a change is necessary in the way we approach preaching and teaching about the Cross in our broader Church theology. As a quick aside, I also believe this change is necessary to establish the present truth in this area and bring forth the restitution of all things (Acts 3:21). Here are the basics of a renewed belief system in the area of healing in light of the aforementioned thought process:

1) If you believe that we have a right through the blood of Jesus to have our sins forgiven every time we ask, then you must also believe that we have a right to have our bodies healed every time we ask, because they were paid for with the same sacrifice. It's a Package Deal!

2) If we are committed to preaching the remission of sins for salvation, then we must also be committed to preach the healing of our bodies, because it was the same Jesus on Calvary that paid for them both, at the same time. It's a Package Deal!

3) How often should we expect to be healed in our bodies? Well, how often do we expect God to forgive us of our sins? It is the same blood of Jesus that washes them both away. It's a Package Deal.

4) If you have faith that God can and will forgive anyone, no matter what they have done, if they

accept Christ, then we must also believe that God will heal anyone no matter the disease, if they accept the free sacrifice of Christ to bare and carry away our diseases. It's a Package Deal!

5) The reason why there are not many miracles of healing in our churches is because we have not committed the resources to teach about healing that we have committed to teach about the forgiveness of sins. When we respect the slain life of Christ to secure our healing with the same faith to wipe away our sins, then we will experience the presence of God to heal more consistently in our Churches. It's that simple. It's a Package Deal!

There are several Scriptures in the NT that show that Jesus Himself honored the benefits of healing the inner and outer man. Here is one from Matthew:

> *And He entered into a ship, and passed over, and came into His own city. And, behold, they brought to Him a man sick of the palsy, lying on a bed: and Jesus seeing their faith said unto the sick of the palsy; Son, be of good cheer;* **thy sins be forgiven thee***. And, behold, certain of the scribes said within themselves, This man blasphemeth. And Jesus knowing their thoughts said, Wherefore think ye evil in your hearts? For whether is easier, to say, Thy sins be forgiven thee; or to say, Arise, and walk?* **But that ye may know that the Son of man hath power on earth to forgive sins,** *(then saith He to the sick of the palsy,) Arise, take up thy bed, and go unto thine house.* **And he arose,** *and departed to his house. (Matthew 9:1-7, emphasis added)*

> *And Jesus went about all the cities and villages, teaching in their synagogues, and* **preaching the gospel of the**

kingdom, and healing every sickness and every disease among the people. (*Matthew 9:35, emphasis added*)

Jesus came to heal the total man: the physical and spiritual man. He came to heal the inner and outer man. Our God is a Total Healing God.

- Chapter 3 -
The Power of Communion:
Why We Must Accept Physical Healing, Too!

Then Jesus said unto them, Verily, verily, I say unto you, Except ye eat the flesh of the Son of man, and drink His blood, ye have no life in you. Whoso eateth My flesh, and drinketh My blood, hath eternal life; and I will raise him up at the last day. For My flesh is meat indeed, and My blood is drink indeed. He that eateth My flesh, and drinketh My blood, dwelleth in Me, and I in him. As the living Father hath sent Me, and I live by the Father: so He that eateth Me, even He shall live by Me. This is that bread which came down from heaven: not as your fathers did eat manna, and are dead: He that eateth of this Bread shall live for ever. These things said He in the synagogue, as He taught in Capernaum. (John 6:53-59)

Communion represents partaking of the body and blood of Jesus Christ. We are introduced to this direct truth by Paul the apostle:

"The cup of blessing which we bless, is it not the communion of the blood of Christ? The bread which we break, is it not the communion of the body of Christ? For

we being many are one bread, and one body: for we are all partakers of that one Bread." (1 Corinthians 10:16-17)

Now, without going into a deep dissertation, the simple question is, "What is the purpose of Communion and what, if anything, is its connection to healing?" (which so happens to be the subject of this book). Glad you asked! Well, the body and blood of Jesus Christ are the quintessential cornerstone of the gospel. We all understand quite simply that our Lord gave His life for us on the Cross of Calvary on Golgotha's hill that we might be saved. No Evangelical would disagree with that! Where we part ways is whether or not physical healing is necessary or essential to the Gospel of Jesus Christ. The subject of communion also answers that question.

Let us consider another familiar passage:

Now in this that I declare unto you, I praise you not, that ye come together not for the better, but for the worse. For first of all, when ye come together in the church, I hear that there be divisions among you; and I partly believe it. For there must be also heresies among you, that they which are approved may be made manifest among you. When ye come together therefore into one place, this is not to eat the Lord's supper. For in eating, every one taketh before other his own supper: and one is hungry, and another is drunken. What? have ye not houses to eat and to drink in? or despise ye the church of God, and shame them that have not? What shall I say to you? shall I praise you in this? I praise you not. For I have received of the Lord that which also I delivered unto you, that the Lord Jesus, the same night in which He was betrayed, took bread: And when He had given thanks, He brake it, and said, Take, eat: this is My body, which is broken for you: this do in remembrance of Me. After the same manner also, He took the cup, when He had supped, saying, This cup is the new testament in My blood: this do ye, as oft as ye drink it, in remembrance of Me. For as often as ye eat this bread, and drink this cup, ye do shew the Lord's death till He come. (1 Corinthians 11:17-26)

To correctly understand this passage, we must revert to the mindset of the Jewish culture and the Christians of the First Century Church. The early Christians did not take communion as a separate ceremony during a Church service; they attended at a Church building every 7 days. They ate unleavened bread and drank wine as part of their normal meal, in addition to eating other foods (which most likely also included kosher goat, lamb, fruit and vegetables). This is also the very reason it is called "The Lord's Supper." It was actually a meal they ate at supper time.

The problem here is that some of God's people were abusing the bread and wine – the Lord's Supper – during this feast. They were abusing it for the same reason most people do today. Simply, by the time supper arrives, we are very hungry and do not want to wait for others to get their food while we ensure we are getting our fair share. (Sound familiar?) Here in Corinthians, Paul admonishes God's people not to do this, due to the sanctity of the Lord's meal. He simply tells them that they have their own homes where they can eat and there is no need to abuse the Lord's Supper during the assembly of the saints while trying to get their bellies full.

After this, we are told very simply the purpose for communion. We are to eat the bread (the body of the Lord Jesus) and drink the cup of wine (His blood) to remember

His death (on the Cross) until He comes again (in celebration of His resurrection).

So what is the problem?

Partaking Unworthily

After we get the purpose, we are hit with a disclaimer, a word of caution on the label – isn't this how it always happens?! (For example: You can get rid of fibromyalgia by taking this drug, but you may also experience dizziness, diarrhea, vomiting and near death as a side effect). Don't you just love those commercials! Sorry, I digress. Here goes the real warning label:

> *Wherefore, whosoever shall eat this bread, and drink this cup of the Lord, **unworthily,** shall be guilty of the body and blood of the Lord. But let a man examine himself, and so let him eat of that bread, and drink of that cup. For he that eateth and drinketh **unworthily**, eateth and drinketh damnation to himself, not discerning the Lord's body. **For this cause many are weak and sickly among you, and many sleep.** For if we would judge ourselves, we should not be judged. But when we are judged, we are chastened of the Lord, that we should not be condemned with the world. (1 Corinthians 11:27-32, emphasis added)*

Now, the disclaimer is quite simple. We are told not to partake of the Lord's body and blood **unworthily.** The cost of partaking unworthily is that we will be damned. Damnation here means a condemnation, judgement, sentencing or penalty. It means that we will pay the price for making the wrong decision. Why? For what decision, exactly, are we being told we will be penalized or pay a price? We are told our crime very simply; it is "NOT DISCERNING THE LORD'S BODY!"

The question then is: "What about the Lord's body are we not discerning?" The word discerning means *understanding*. We are being condemned because we do not UNDERSTAND the Lord's body. And what should be our understanding of His body? Well, we have already learned this:

> *Surely, He hath borne our griefs, and carried our sorrows: yet we did esteem Him stricken, smitten of God, and afflicted. But He was wounded for our transgressions, He was bruised for our iniquities: the chastisement of our peace was upon Him; and with His stripes, we are healed. (Isaiah 53:4-5)*

This Scripture tells us what we should understand concerning Christ and His body. He gave His life for us. He died for us! He shed His blood for us! The result of His sacrifice is that by His stripes, we are healed! Everyone knows that.

Now, how do we know that this is a contextually congruent thought? What do the Scriptures say is the penalty or price for eating and drinking damnation unto oneself? I mean, what will actually happen to me if I commit this sin? Well, the Bible tells us this way. It says:

> *For this cause, many are weak and sickly among you, and many sleep. (1 Corinthians 11:30)*

Whaaaaaaaaaaaaaaaaat?! What were we just told? We were just told the cost, penalty and sentence for not understanding the Lord's body. That's what we were just told. We have found that there are three basic things that can happen to a person for the sin of partaking of the Lord's body and blood unworthily, *without understanding it*. There are the 3 basic categories, in purposeful order of their severity:

1) Many are weak: constantly exhausted, stressed out, lacking will and strength, feeble, impotent.
2) Many are sickly: infirmed with sickness or disease, in a constant state of pain or anxiety.
3) Many sleep: have passed away and are physically dead before their appointed time.

This makes perfect sense. If we do not remember what the Lord accomplished with His death until He comes again, and do not take heed that He died so we might be healed, it makes sense that we might become physically weak or sick or end up passing away before our time. This is the very goal of the law of sin and death! It makes perfect sense that these things may happen if we forget that Jesus Christ died to prevent them from happening.

This is exactly what we have done in the modern Church. We have separated physical healing from the Gospel of Jesus Christ. We have refused to understand the Lord's body until He comes again. We have removed physical healing as a necessity of the Cross. We have made it an optional ordinance. We no longer take communion with the faith expectation that we should be physically healed by the sacrifice of our King. The result is quite glaring: we become weak, sick and die, in that order. This should not be. This is not what Jesus meant for us. This is not why He gave His life. He came that we might have life and have it more abundantly (John 10:10). We are not supposed to be weak, but strong. We are not supposed to be sick, but healed. We are not supposed to die prematurely, but live abundantly.

- Part 2 -
Healing & Miraculous Powers

The Revelation of Healing

- Chapter 4 -
The Power to Heal

The four Gospels are heavy laden with examples of Jesus' healing ministry. Jesus was in the healing business. But how? How did the Master heal? What was the source of His healing power? More practically, how did He and His disciples actually perform signs, wonders, and miracles? How did they cast out demons? How did they command sickness to flee?

It seems difficult to understand how Jesus and His disciples performed the miracles and executed the healings. This is the conversation I want to begin in this chapter. I want us to move from spectators of the works of Jesus to participants. First, let us discuss the source of Jesus' miracle working powers. As always, our answer is in the Word of God:

And a woman having an issue of blood twelve years, which had spent all her living upon physicians, neither could be healed of any, came behind Him, and touched the border of His garment: immediately her issue of blood stanched. And Jesus said, Who touched Me? When all denied, Peter and they that were with Him said, Master, the multitude throng Thee and press Thee, and sayest Thou, Who touched Me? And Jesus said, Somebody hath touched Me:

*for I perceive that **virtue** [**dunamis**] is gone out of Me. (Luke 8:43-48, emphasis added)*

Within this Scripture, much is exposed. Mainly, the source of Jesus' healing power: **virtue**. The word "virtue" here is found to be that well studied Greek word *dunamis*. We know *dunamis* to be defined as miraculous power, force or might, like dynamite or explosive power. Jesus feels this power leave His physical body when the woman having an issue of blood touches the hem of His garment. Jesus' feels virtue – or power – literally leave His body. And thus is revealed the basic physics of healing. Power must leave the healer's body and be released to the person needing the healing. Like all power, it will take the path of least resistance and go where there is a deficiency in the system. In this example, the diseased body of the woman with the issue of blood provides this need. She simply completes the circuit by touching the border of His garment and *KABOOM* – she is healed.

This story is very significant, because it shows us the concept of power transfer in the healing process. We now know what we are seeking in the process.

Now, how do we get involved? We know Jesus can do it, but what is our part in the Kingdom? Do we have access to the same source? Here goes:

*But **ye** [you] shall receive **power** [**dunamis**], after that **the Holy Ghost is come upon you:** and ye shall be witnesses unto Me both in Jerusalem, and in all Judea, and in Samaria, and unto the uttermost part of the earth. (Acts 1:8, emphasis added)*

Yes, Jesus provides His early disciples with the same power to heal. They are given the power of the Holy Ghost.

He is our power source. And it just so happens that the Holy Ghost and His power are available to every Believer:

*Then Peter said unto them, Repent, and be baptized every one of you in the Name of Jesus Christ for the remission of sins, and ye shall receive the gift of the Holy Ghost. For the promise is unto you, and to your children, and to all that are afar off, **even as many as the Lord our God shall call.** (Acts 2:38-39, emphasis added)*

And these signs shall follow them that believe; In My Name shall they cast out devils; they shall speak with new tongues; they shall take up serpents; and if they drink any deadly thing, it shall not hurt them; they shall lay hands on the sick, and they shall recover. (Mark 16:17-18)

What? know ye not that your body is the temple of the Holy Ghost which is in you, which ye have of God, and ye are not your own? For ye are bought with a price: therefore glorify God in your body, and in your spirit, which are God's. (1 Corinthians 6:19-20)

This means that we have access to the same power that Jesus Christ used to perform signs, wonders, healings and deliverances. This is very important! It brings light to many other Scriptures throughout the Bible that we have read. Here is an example:

Verily, verily, I say unto you, He that believeth on Me, the works that I do shall He do also; and greater works than these shall he do; because I go unto My Father. (John 14:12)

It makes no sense for Jesus to tell His disciples that they will do the same works He can do (*e.g.*, physical healings, casting out of demons, changing water to wine, *etc.*) if they do not have access to the same power He exhibited. If being

Jesus is a requirement to do what Jesus did in the Scriptures, then it would not make sense for our Lord to say that others can duplicate His works, much less do greater works than these. Understanding that Jesus healed by the Power of the Holy Ghost clears up this issue, because we are promised to receive the same Spirit when we accept Jesus Christ. This also explains why our Lord expected these signs to follow any that believed (Mark 16:17-18).

In fact, all the signs, wonders, miracles, healings and deliverances that Jesus performed were done solely by the power of the Holy Spirit. Jesus Himself stated the source of His power and how He did the works His Father sent Him to do. He said:

> *The Spirit of the Lord is upon Me, because He hath anointed Me to preach the gospel to the poor; He hath sent Me to heal the brokenhearted, to preach deliverance to the captives, and recovering of sight to the blind, to set at liberty them that are bruised, to preach the acceptable year of the Lord. (Luke 4:18-19)*

Though simple, this is very significant, because it provides insight into how Jesus has given us access to the same power He used in His ministry, the Holy Spirit. In fact, it explains why He left us the Comforter in the first place, to do what He would do as if He were here (John 14:25-26). This why we have so many examples of His healing ministry, to read them and have an expectation that we can duplicate them later.

In fact, it is not a coincidence that Healing and Miracles are two of the 9 gifts of the Holy Spirit in 1 Corinthians 12:7-11:

1) Word of wisdom
2) Word of knowledge
3) Faith
4) **Gifts of healing**
5) **Working (*energema*) of miracles (*dunamis*)**
6) Prophecy
7) Discerning of spirits
8) Divers kinds of tongues
9) Interpretation of tongues

Jesus came to defeat sin and death so that every Believer can have access to the nine gifts of the Holy Spirit. These are not all of the gifts (or manifestations) of the Holy Spirit in the Scriptures. But they are the only gifts of the Spirit to which every Believer has access. (I will explain this in a later chapter on Prophetic Healing Teams.) This is also why Jesus had an expectation that signs would follow every Believer, because He planned to give every Believer access to all nine of these gifts.

Before I move to discuss how to release the *dunamis* power of the Holy Ghost in the same manner as Jesus released it, I want to talk a bit more about why we should have an expectation to do the things that Jesus was able to do in the Scriptures in the next chapter.

- Chapter 5 -
What Manner of Man is This?

One of the main reasons why God came to earth as a man was to show man what He can do by faith. Many Christians have a hard time accepting this truth because they insist on believing that all the mighty works which Jesus did were possible only because He was God. There is no mighty work which Jesus administered that necessitated Him being God to perform. All of the miracles which Jesus worked are possible by any being made in the image and likeness of God, formed by the dust of the earth.

The difference between Christ and the other miracle working men of the Scriptures is that they were born into sin and Jesus was not. Not only was Jesus not born into sin, but He was born of the Holy Ghost. He was the Word of God manifested in the flesh (John 1:14). But, to say that Jesus' ability to perform miracles is evidence that He was God makes no Biblical sense, for this criterion also qualifies many of the OT prophets and patriarchs as God, and they clearly were NOT! Jesus' ability to work miracles did not even cause the Pharisees and teachers of the Law to consider Jesus as God. This only caused them to parallel Him with the prophets of the OT who also worked miracles (John 16:13-14).

The quintessential truth that made Jesus special above all other men that have ever graced the earth was that He was without sin. This is the manner of man Jesus represented. He was a man born and filled with the Holy Ghost, yet without sin. This is an entirely different species of man. There is no other man who has ever walked the face of the earth that can boast having this feature. It is not Christ's healing, working of miracles, ability to teach with authority, great love and compassion, or any other thing that set Him apart. All of these other things can be done and have been done by other men.

The Image and Likeness of Jesus Christ

Christ's ability to walk in the supernatural power of God, however, opened the gateway for an entirely new species of mankind to be born. Adam led one lineage of mankind and Jesus started an entirely new species of men. Consider the following Scriptures:

> But as many as received Him, to them gave He power to become the sons of God, even to them that believe on His Name: which were born, not of blood, nor of the will of the flesh, nor of the will of man, but of God. (John 1:13-14)

> For as by one man's disobedience many were made sinners, so by the obedience of One shall many be made righteous. (Romans 5:19)

> For whom he did foreknow, he also did predestinate to be conformed to the image of his Son, that he might be the firstborn among many brethren. Moreover whom he did predestinate, them he also called: and whom he called, them he also justified: and whom he justified, them he also glorified. (Romans 8:29-30)

Therefore, if any man be in Christ, he is a new creature: old things are passed away; behold, all things are become new. (2 Corinthians 5:17)

Adam, the first man, was made in the image and likeness of God (Genesis 1:27). When Adam fell in the Garden of Eden, he introduced sin and death into the race of mankind (Romans 5:12).

Because all men are made in the image and likeness of Adam through birth, all men after Adam were subject to sin and death (Genesis 5:3-32). Adam birthed a race of sinners. This race of sinning men had all the rights of Adam, to rule and reign on the earth (Genesis 1:28). When Jesus was born, He became the first man of an entirely new species of men. Those who receive Jesus are born again after the image and likeness of Jesus Christ. Jesus is the father of the righteous. This new race of righteous men are born with all the rights and privileges of Jesus Christ, the Son of God (John 1:12). They can rule and reign on the earth just as Jesus demonstrated.

This begs the question: if we are born again after the likeness of Jesus Christ, why do we keep sinning after the likeness of Adam? The answer is simple: when we are born again, our spirit man is born again, and our natural man is not. Our natural man is still made in the image and likeness of Adam, the man of sin, even after we accept Christ. When men die, they are separated from their natural body. If they have been born again, their spirit man will be with God for an eternity and will receive a new spiritual body (1 Corinthians 15:35-45).

- Chapter 6 -
Healing by NOW Faith

Before we go much further, it is necessary to define more definitively how healing and miraculous powers work. To do that, it is necessary to put some meat on the subject of faith. In most of Jesus' healing exercises in the Gospels, He was clear to state that, in pursuit of healing, it is faith that makes us whole. Healing works through faith.

Fortunately for me, I have already written a pretty good book on faith (if I must say so myself) called <u>The Revelation of Faith: Overcoming Fear & Unbelief</u>, and therefore, I will not venture to explain every nook and cranny of the subject in this chapter. However, if you feel you need a review, by all means, feel free to get a copy online (available through Amazon).

With that said, I would like to start from Jesus' simple definition in the Book of Mark about how faith is activated:

And Jesus answering saith unto them, Have faith in God. For verily I say unto you, that whosoever shall say unto this mountain, Be thou removed, and be thou cast into the sea; and shall not doubt in his heart, but shall believe that those things which he saith shall come to pass; he shall have whatsoever he saith. Therefore I say unto you, What things

*soever ye desire, when ye pray, believe that ye receive them,
and ye shall have them. (Mark 11:22-24)*

We can now understand what Jesus taught about faith.
It has a few simple principles that are necessary for it to be
effective:

1) Faith starts in the heart, we must believe what we
   say "shall come to pass"!
2) Faith is released from our mouths when we speak
   "To" something (*i.e.,* "whosoever shall say unto this
   mountain").
3) The process of believing and speaking is called
   "prayer."
4) We are to believe we receive the result of our prayer
   of faith "at the time we are praying" and not
   afterward (*i.e.,* "when ye pray, believe that ye
   receive them").

This is the specific concept the Bible calls the prayer of
faith. We get this concept by combining verses 22 and 24
together. Verse 22 is about 'faith' and verse 24 is about
'prayer'. Verse 23, therefore, is defining the 'prayer of faith.'
With this understanding we can also derive the following
concepts of the prayer of faith more clearly:

1) The prayer of faith is not a request, it is a decree. We
   are to speak directly "TO" not "ABOUT" the
   mountain (Mark 11:23).
2) The prayer of faith is executed in the NOW (Hebrew
   11:1).
3) The prayer of faith is a prayer of Effect. We are to
   look for a change in the mountain "when we pray"
   (Mark 11:24).

4) We are to invoke change in the mountain by speaking (*i.e.*, "Be thou removed, and be thou cast into the sea") (Mark 11:23).
5) We pray (speak by faith) until the spiritual gift of faith is fully manifested and COMPLETED (Mark 8:22-25, 1 Corinthians 12:9).

There are two very good examples of the prayer of faith in action in the Scriptures. One is given by Jesus' brother James and the other is given by Jesus Himself. Let's first look at the example given by James.

The Prayer of Faith Defined

*Is any among you afflicted? Let him pray. Is any merry? Let him sing psalms. Is any sick among you? Let him call for the elders of the church; and let them pray over him, anointing him with oil in the Name of the Lord: And **the prayer of faith** shall save the sick, and the Lord shall raise him up; and if he have committed sins, they shall be forgiven him. Confess your faults one to another, and pray one for another, that ye may be healed. **The effectual fervent prayer of a righteous man availeth much.** Elias was a man subject to like passions as we are, and **he prayed earnestly** that it might not rain: and it rained not on the earth by the space of three years and six months. And **he prayed again**, and the heaven gave rain, and the earth brought forth her fruit. (James 5:13-18, emphasis added)*

Wow, I can't wait to unpack this for you!

It's Going to Rain

To understand how the prayer of faith works, in the context of healing, James the brother of Jesus, tells us we must look at the example of Elijah, the prophet. Before telling us how Elijah used the prayer of faith, he makes sure to show us, first, that Elijah was "a man of like passions as we are." We are given this tidbit of information to help us get past the elephant in the room.

Mainly, James wants us to get past the thought that Elijah was a great prophet of God, and of course, most of us will think we are not great prophets, at least not at the same level Elijah operated. When was the last time you rained down fire from heaven with your faith? James, the writer, knows this fact, and is making sure we do not use this stumbling block to miss how Elijah used the basic principles of the prayer of faith to do something miraculous for God. James wants us to know that Elijah was not a better man being than we are, and therefore, if Elijah could do it, if we use the same faith principles, we can get the same results. Elijah was hindered by the same desires of the flesh to which we are subject as Christians today, yet he still successfully used the prayer of faith.

What is the prayer of faith? James defines the prayer of faith as the effectual fervent prayer of a righteous man (male or female, of course). He tells us that this kind of prayer will 'avail much,' meaning the prayer of faith will have power and force to do extraordinary deeds. We are also told the prayer of faith is effectual. This simply means that the prayer of faith will have the power to 'effect change' in the thing we are praying to come to pass. We should have an expectation that this kind of prayer will make a difference, and will not allow a thing to stay the same way it was previous to our prayer.

Now, how specifically did the prophet Elijah use the prayer of faith? We are told two basic facts:

1) Elijah **prayed earnestly** that it might not rain: and it rained not on the earth by the space of three years and six months,
2) Elijah **prayed again,** and the heaven gave rain, and the earth brought forth her fruit.

What we are not given here is a specific record of Elijah's prayer, so we can see exactly how it was executed. Fortunately, we have been given this account in 1 Kings chapters 17 & 18 to see exactly how it happened.

Here is the exact account – no more, no less.

To Stop the Rain:

And Elijah the Tishbite, who was of the inhabitants of Gilead, said unto Ahab, As the LORD God of Israel liveth, before whom I stand, there shall not be dew nor rain these years, but according to my word. (1 Kings 17:1)

To Restart the Rain:

And it came to pass after many days, that the word of the LORD came to Elijah in the third year, saying, Go, shew thyself unto Ahab; and I will send rain upon the earth. (1 Kings 18:1)

And Elijah said unto Ahab, Get thee up, eat and drink; for there is a sound of abundance of rain. So Ahab went up to eat and to drink. And Elijah went up to the top of Carmel; and he cast himself down upon the earth, and put his face between his knees, And said to his servant, Go up now, look toward the sea. And he went up, and looked, and said, There is nothing. And he said, Go again seven times. And it came to pass at the seventh time, that he said, Behold, there ariseth a little cloud out of the sea, like a man's hand. And he said, Go up, say unto Ahab, Prepare thy chariot, and get thee down, that the rain stop thee not. And it came to pass in the mean while, that the heaven was black with clouds and wind, and there was a great rain. And Ahab rode, and went to Jezreel. (1 Kings 18:41-46)

Now, that's it! That's how it went down. You are free to read chapters 17 and 18 in their entirety to see if there was more to it (by all means be thorough). However, I have already done that for us and you will see that his prayer is as simple as you have read it (above).

Now, I would like to bring to your attention, not so much the things that Elijah does during his prayer of faith, but the things that Elijah does NOT do during the prayer:

1) At no time does Elijah make a request during this prayer to stop the rain. He does not say, "If it be Thy will, Oh God, please stop the rain."
2) At no time does Elijah get down on his knees to petition heaven to stop the rain.
3) At no time does Elijah pray ABOUT the rain. There is no long prayer dissertation in which Elijah begins to pray ABOUT his desire to stop the rain.

What does occur? I'm glad you asked. What happens is that Elijah speaks directly TO King Ahab and tells him the word of the Lord concerning his situation. He declares to King Ahab that it will not rain again, except according to his (Elijah's) WORD. Are you getting this? Elijah's prayer is not a request, it is a declaration! The prayer of faith is not a request; we are not asking for anything. It is a DECLARATION. It is a DECREE. The prayer of faith is not praying ABOUT anything, it is speaking directly TO something or someone.

This is consistent with Jesus' definition we learned earlier concerning the prayer of faith:

For verily I say unto you, that whosoever shall say unto this mountain, Be thou removed, and be thou cast into the sea; and shall not doubt in his heart, but shall believe that those things which he saith shall come to pass; he shall have whatsoever he saith. (Mark 11:23)

We can also see that Elijah gets it to rain again by similarly speaking directly to King Ahab and speaking directly into the rain situation. I want to repeat: at no time do we see Elijah get down on his knees and pray to the Father in heaven to petition Him to stop or start the rain. To get the rain to start again, Elijah receives a Word from the Lord (a *rhema* word that we will define in Chapter 9). Elijah used this Word to get down on his knees before the Father in heaven. Even then, he does not petition heaven to make it rain again. He stays on his knees and tells his servant to go up and look toward the sea until he sees evidence of rain. He tells his servant to do this seven times, until he sees some evidence that his decree is effective.

What is Elijah seeking while he is executing the prayer of faith? He is looking for the effect of his prayer to take place. He does not get up from his knees until he has evidence that his prayer of faith is working. This is effect(ual) fervent prayer. It is making a decree by faith that will move the mountain right at the time, while we are praying.

This is the difference between traditional prayer, which is a request or petition to heaven, and the prayer of faith, which is a declaration or decree. What we know as traditional prayer is a petition to heaven, we are asking God the Father to do something for us. We are praying ABOUT something or someone. However, the prayer of faith is speaking to something or someone (Jesus called this a

51

mountain in His example). This kind of effectual fervent prayer is executed when we speak directly TO – NOT ABOUT – something. Our expectation is that the thing TO which we are speaking will move, at that moment (while) we are speaking TO it. This is why it is a prayer of EFFECT, because we expect to see the result while (or at least very shortly after) we are speaking to it.

Now, let me be clear here. I am not saying there is anything wrong with the way we have been taught to pray traditionally, which is a prayer of request to the Father in heaven. There are plenty of Scriptures in the Bible that support the idea that this is a correct way to pray. I am in no way saying that you should not pray ABOUT something or someone. However, doing this is NOT the prayer of faith.

Furthermore, it is not the kind of prayer we are taught brings forth healing in the Scriptures. When we see Jesus or His disciples perform a healing in the Scriptures, it is always executed by a prayer of faith. Meaning, Jesus or one of His many disciples, speaks directly to the person or thing needing to be healed. And not by coincidence, you will find the exception to this to be that Jesus will use the words of the person that needs the healing, only because that person spoke directly TO this situation, before Jesus got the opportunity to speak TO it Himself.

As I told you before, there are 2 very good examples of the prayer of faith in action in the Scriptures. One is given by Jesus' brother James and the other is given by Jesus Himself. Let's take a look at the second example given by Jesus.

All Men are as Trees

*And He cometh to Bethsaida; and they bring a blind man unto Him, and besought Him to touch him. And He took the blind man by the hand, and led him out of the town; and when He had spit on his eyes, and **put His hands upon him, He asked him if he saw ought**. And he looked up, and said, **I see men as trees, walking**. After that **He put His hands again** upon his eyes, and made him look up: and **he was restored, and saw every man clearly**. And He sent him away to his house, saying, Neither go into the town, nor tell it to any in the town. (Mark 8:22-26, emphasis added)*

I love this story. It is a simple one if we can accept what we are reading.

Here we find the prayer of faith in action, mixed with the laying on of hands. The perfect healing combo! [We will speak more about the doctrine of laying on of hands in the next chapter]. Once again, someone in need of healing finds Jesus. Jesus takes him out of the town to perform the cure (probably so some religious person does not use their unbelief to mess up the healing). Jesus spits on his eyes (using a Word of Wisdom) and lays hands on the man. He does not stop to pray a traditional prayer, asking the Father in heaven if it is His will to heal the man. Instead, Jesus speaks directly to the man and asks him if he sees anything.

In response, we find the most awesome example of the effective (effectual) fervent prayer. The man says, "I see men as trees." In other words, I am not still blind, but I am not 100% healed. Now, why does Jesus stop to ask the man if he sees anything? Jesus is looking for the EFFECT of his prayer of faith, because it is a prayer of CAUSE and EFFECT. The cause is faith. The effect is the healing. We find that even

Jesus was bound by the laws of effect when using the prayer of faith, for the healing was not completely successful the first time. Did you see what the Scriptures just showed us? Even Jesus was not always completely successful when He used His faith the first time.

However, Jesus did not give up on the healing business. He did not suddenly declare that it must not be the Father's will to heal in this scenario. What did Jesus do? Very simply, HE PUT HIS HANDS AGAIN UPON HIS EYES. The effect was that he saw every man clearly!

So, let's review! The prayer of faith is a cause and effect kind of prayer. It is not a prayer of petition or request, but a prayer of declaration or decree. When we pray the prayer of faith, we are not praying ABOUT something or someone, we are speaking TO something or someone. We are to speak TO our mountains and not pray ABOUT them. When we do this, our prayers will be effectual and fervent, causing them to avail much. This means our prayers will have the power to do the things Jesus and His many disciples did, and greater things than these will we be capable of doing (John 14:12).

As promised, let's learn about the doctrine of laying on of hands in the next chapter.

- Chapter 7 -
The Laying On of Hands:
Releasing the *Dunamis* Power of God

The reason that many men of God do not believe in the laying on of hands is because they rationalize, "What if the power of God to heal the sick or impart wisdom does not show up when I lay hands on His people?" They reason that it is impractical to lay hands or believe in the miraculous because it may cause people to have a false security about their situation, not knowing they are walking away the same way they came to the alter. They reason that people will call them false teachers, *etc.*, if people do not get healed immediately after the laying on of hands is administered.

Some believe that there is no power in the laying on of hands today, as there was in Bible times. They believe that men do not have power in today's Church through hands laying and that only God directly heals the sick. They argue that it is not guaranteed that anyone will be healed through the laying on of hands, and therefore, there is no practical reason to do it, because it only leaves people disappointed when they are still sick and still in need of healing. They believe that God heals only whom He wants and not whomever we choose to lay on our hands by the power that works within us.

Despite these arguments, there are direct promises and commands from the Scriptures to lay on hands:

And these signs shall follow them that believe... they shall lay hands on the sick, and they shall recover (Mark 16:17a, 18c)

Is any sick among you? let him call for the elders of the church, and let them pray over him, anointing him with oil in the Name of the Lord: and the prayer of faith shall save the sick, and the Lord shall raise him up; and if he hath committed sins, they shall be forgiven him. (James 5:14-15)

It is my belief that we should spend less time analyzing why God does not do certain things and more time carrying out the things God has commanded us to do. I do not know why the sick are not healed instantaneously every time hands are laid on them. Quite frankly, I am not convinced this should be our concern. Our job as elders is to anoint with oil and to lay hands on the sick. Our job is to execute the Word of God; He has promised to do the rest. I have not read in the Scriptures where God intended for the sick to no longer recover by miraculous healings after the days of the apostles and the early Church. If we are Believers, and Jesus said these signs will follow them that believe, I find it hard to believe that Jesus' words were attached with an expiration date.

There are many things in the Scriptures that many theologians claim are no longer needed in today's Church: prophecy, laying on of hands, anointing with oil, speaking in unknown tongues, the working of miracles, interpretation of tongues, *etc.* They claim that these things died out with the early Church and its apostles. Yet, I find it strange that we are diligent to keep some of the other works of the Church without any similar struggle.

I have noticed that all things that the Bible teaches us to observe that cannot be comprehended by the mind have been deemed as "no longer needed in the Church." I have also noticed that the traditions of the Scriptures that men perceive to be easily comprehendible are continued and cherished by the Church.

For example, the traditions of Jesus and His disciples of water baptism and communion are, for the most part, observed by all denominations of churches. How to perform these sacraments is relatively spelled out step-by-step in the Scriptures. Anyone – the faithful or faithless – can carry out these rituals, because they are generally perceived to be comprehendible. Though many debate with what piety, method or solemnness these sacraments should be administered, few debate whether they should be continued in today's Church.

On the other hand, there are other traditions of Christ and His disciples that are highly debated in the Church: speaking in tongues, prophets and prophecy, the laying on of hands, and the working of miracles by men. Though you may not agree with my theology, at least admit that this is an interesting observation, one that deserves further study.

Making the Connection

The logical reason for the laying on of hands is quite simple, really. As discussed in Chapter 4, the *dunamis* power of God is necessary to bring about healing. That virtue is transferred from the body of the healer to the body of the person needing the healing. The natural way, though not the only way to do this, is to touch another person with one's hand to start the transfer of power, like a connection being closed in a circuit. Simply, healing power is available in the body of the healer, he reaches forth his hand to touch the body of the sick. Power is released from point A to point B. The power destroys the sickness or disease. The sick person is healed, either immediately or shortly thereafter. This is our Scriptural expectation, by faith.

[Let me park here, parenthetically, to explain my use of the term *dunamis* power. Etymologically speaking, do not be alarmed. I know that I am saying "power-power." I have chosen to use the English language in this way, much the same as we use it when saying *chai tea*. Chai is the Swahili word for tea. Technically speaking, here, we are saying "tea-tea." (A Kenyan child very matter-of-factly revealed this to my wife and me while we were in Kenya, a former English Colony.) However, when saying "chai tea," we differentiate what kind of tea we are describing when ordering this beverage among other kinds of tea in our American culture. Consequently, no one complains about saying "chai tea" when standing in line at Dunkin' Donuts or Starbucks. It is now a cultural norm. It is with this same spirit that I use the phrase *"dunamis* power" in this book. I am simply specifying what kind of power I am discussing, the healing power of God that comes from the Holy Ghost. That said, please pardon my use of this redundant phrase, as it is used for understandings sake throughout this text.]

Having said that, we cannot operate in the Church without His *dunamis* power. *Dunamis* power is the essential ingredient to the work of the Church today. Without it, the Church is truly powerless to bring about the restitution of all things (Acts 3:21). We are salt that has lost its saltiness (Matthew 5:13-16). We are a like a city on a hill, trying to hide ourselves. We are a candle under a bushel. We have a form of godliness but are denying its power (2 Timothy 3:5).

There are many examples of the laying on of hands to release the *dunamis* power of God in the Scriptures. Here are a few for your consideration:

*And it came to pass, when He was in a certain city, behold a man full of leprosy: who seeing Jesus, fell on his face, and besought Him, saying, Lord, if Thou wilt, Thou canst make me clean. **And He put forth His hand, and touched him,** saying, I will: be thou clean. And immediately the leprosy departed from him. (Luke 5:12-13, emphasis added)*

*And He was teaching in one of the synagogues on the sabbath. And behold, there was a woman which had a spirit of infirmity eighteen years, and was bowed together, and could in no wise lift up herself. And when Jesus saw her, He called her to Him, and said unto her, Woman, thou are loosed from thy infirmity. **And He laid His hands on her:** and immediately she was made straight, and glorified God. (Luke 13:10-13, emphasis added)*

Now, Peter and John went up together into the temple at the hour of prayer, being the ninth hour. And a certain man lame from his mother's womb was carried, whom they laid daily at the gate of the temple which is called Beautiful, to ask alms of them that entered into the temple; who seeing Peter and John about to go into the temple asked an alms. And Peter, fastening his eyes upon him with John, said, Look on us. And he gave heed unto them, expecting to receive something of them. Then Peter said, Silver and gold have I none; but such as I have give I thee: In the Name of Jesus Christ of Nazareth, rise up and walk. **And he took him by the right hand, and lifted him up:** *and immediately his feet and ankle bones received strength. (Acts 3:1-7, emphasis added)*

The laying on of hands is used in the Scriptures to transfer power, authority and blessings in both the OT and NT. Jacob blessed the sons of Joseph and blessed them to be a great multitude through the laying on of hands (Genesis 48:14-20). Moses laid his hand on Joshua and put his honor upon him in front of the nation of Israel and Eleazar the Priest (Numbers 27:18-23). Jesus blessed the little children through the laying on of hands (Mark 10:13-16). Paul laid hands on the disciples at Corinth and they spoke in tongues and prophesied (Acts 19:6). Touch is a point of transfer. The hands represent the natural instrument of touch.

The Bible calls the laying on of hands an elementary doctrine of Christ, meaning this is a basic principle of our faith. It tells us in the book of Hebrews that we should have grown beyond needing to be convinced about this simple truth again:

*Therefore, leaving the principles of the doctrine of Christ, let us go on unto perfection; not laying again the foundation of repentance from dead works, and of faith toward God, of the doctrine of baptisms, **and of laying on of hands,** and of resurrection of the dead, and of eternal judgment. And this will we do, if God permit. (Hebrews 6:1-3, emphasis added)*

In fact, the Bible tells us we should be teaching about these truths by now, but instead need someone to teach us all over again because we are babies (Hebrews 5:11-14).

When I was a teenager, I was greatly convicted by the Holy Spirit about those with sicknesses and diseases. Whenever I would pass someone that was disabled (*e.g.*, in a wheelchair or crutches), I would feel the stirring of the Holy Spirit within me to heal them. I would notice that this power within me would intensify if I chose to walk past a person that was physically disabled in some way. I knew that God wanted me to pray for them to be healed, but I had never done this before and it was not taught at my local church. I wondered what would happen if I laid hands on them and they were not healed. As a result, fear rose up within me and I would ignore the unction of the Holy Spirit.

I would feel my hands heat up whenever I would see someone in need of healing. I knew what God ultimately wanted me to do. I just needed courage to do it. I knew I must overcome the spirit of rejection. In time, I learned to be obedient to the voice of the Holy Spirit within me. The Spirit of God convinced me that it was better to obey His voice, no matter the result. He convinced me to leave the result to Him and to just do my part. The anointing of the Holy Ghost would take care of the rest.

The Lord taught me how to heal small things first, like a fever when someone had the flu or a headache when someone had toxins in their body. He showed me how to overcome the common cold by resisting and rebuking the desire to cough. He even increased my faith by allowing me to heal our family dog, Josiah, when he was at the point of death. Even though I knew I had the power to heal within me, I was still surprised when Josiah actually lived. I can still remember how great it was to feel the healing power of God go from my hand into his frail, slow breathing body. I couldn't believe my Mother asked me to pray for Him. (You rock, Mom!)

The Lord was trying, then, while I was still a teenager, to teach me a simple principle concerning healing. He used this well-known Scripture to do it:

*Withhold not good from them to whom it is due, when it is in the **power of thine hand** to do it. (Proverbs 3:27, emphasis added)*

Though we usually are thinking about money, clothes, food or some other commodity when reading this verse, the Lord used it to teach me a lesson on how His healing power works through the laying on of hands. He taught me that the heat in my hands represented the power of God to heal. The heating of my hands was a sign that God desired to bring forth a healing. He taught me that I had a responsibility to my fellow man not to withhold the gift of healing from him, when it was within the power of my hands to release it. You see, the healing power of God did not belong to me, anyway. It was a gift for the person needing the healing. Who was I to withhold it from them?

In the next chapter, I want to describe from where this heat comes and explore the supernatural realm of the angels.

- Chapter 8 -
The Flames of Fire:
Healing with Angelic Service

But ye are come unto mount Sion, and unto the city of the living God, the heavenly Jerusalem, and to an innumerable company of angels, to the general assembly and church of the firstborn, which are written in heaven, and to God the Judge of all, and to the spirits of just men made perfect, and to Jesus the mediator of the new covenant, and to the blood of sprinkling, that speaketh better things than that of Abel. (Hebrews 12:22-24)

One of the greatest revelations of the Kingdom of God is the relationship between the Church of Jesus Christ and the innumerable company of angels in the spiritual realm. This heavenly host (the angels) has always played a pivotal role in the advancement of the Kingdom of God and His Church. One of the best kept secrets of the Bible is the idea that the angels have been the "Secret Service" of the Kingdom of God and God's representatives since the OT. The angels are the oldest clandestine organization on the planet responsible to protect the government of the Kingdom of Heaven (KOH).

Because the will of the Father in heaven is to cause His Kingdom to come on earth as it is in heaven, it is necessary that the government of heaven assign heavenly angelic resources to ensure that the earth is properly colonized according to the King's will. Also, because mankind has been given dominion over the earth (Genesis 1:26-28), most of those resources have been assigned to strategic members of mankind (*e.g.,* Jacob, Moses, *etc.*) as God has been building His Church since the world began. The idea that angels are assigned to Believers is clearly spelled out in Hebrews chapter 1:

And of the angels He saith, Who maketh His angels spirits, ***and His ministers a flame of fire.*** *(Hebrews 1:7)*

Are they not all ministering spirits, ***sent forth to minister for them who shall be heirs of salvation?*** *(Hebrews 1:14, emphasis added)*

A quick study of Hebrews 1 teaches us that God assigns angels to every Believer, to those that inherit the gift of salvation. The angels here are called flames of fire and ministering spirits. We are told that they are sent to serve (or minister) for them that are heirs of salvation.

This is very important to understand, that God assigned an angel to you the day you accepted Jesus Christ as your Lord and personal Savior. An angel, a flame of fire, was sent to serve your needs, to make sure you reached your destiny in Christ, the day you became an heir of salvation. Are there enough angels to go around? Absolutely, there is an innumerable company of angels in heaven. There is no shortage of heavenly resources.

Now, what is your angel from heaven supposed to help you do, exactly? What is your angel's assignment as a ministering spirit? What is your angel's assignment as a flame of fire? We'll need to go to the next chapter of Hebrews for that answer:

> *Therefore, we ought to give the more earnest heed to the things which we have heard, lest at any time we should let them slip.* **For if the word spoken by angels was stedfast***, and every transgression and disobedience received a just recompense of reward; how shall we escape, if we neglect* **so great salvation***; which at the first began to be spoken by the Lord, and was confirmed unto us by them that heard Him;* **God also bearing them witness, both with signs and wonders, and with divers miracles, and gifts of the Holy Ghost, according to His own will?** *(Hebrews 2:1-4, emphasis added)*

I love these Scriptures! They answer so many unanswered questions.

First, what are the angels supposed to do as they are sent to minister for us that have inherited salvation? The answer: they are supposed to work signs and wonders and diverse miracles. Second, how are we supposed to work signs, wonders and miracles in our generation? The answer: we are not supposed to work signs, wonders and miracles, the angels will do them as they minister for us (Hebrews 1:14). Last, why does the Bible say these signs shall follow them that believe... (Mark 16:17-18). The answer: because the angels are assigned to follow every Believer in Jesus Christ wherever they may go.

We are also shown here that the angels cooperate with us along with the gifts we have been given from the Holy Ghost, the nine gifts of the Holy Spirit (1 Corinthians 12:7-11).

Fire and the Day of Pentecost

So, let's cut to the chase! I believe the day anyone accepts Jesus Christ as his/her Lord and personal Savior and becomes a born-again Believer, two things are supposed to happen:

1) You are supposed to receive the gift of the Holy Ghost (with His nine gifts for every born-again Believer) and His baptism,

2) You are supposed to be assigned an angel, a flame of fire, so that signs will follow your life in the form of speaking a new tongue, rebuking the devil, divine protection, and laying hands on the sick so that they will recover (Mark 16:17-18, paraphrase added).

With the help of a few other witnesses of Scripture, I believe this basic example is set forth on the Day of Pentecost in the book of Acts:

John answered, saying unto them all, I indeed baptize you with water; but One mightier than I cometh, the latchet of Whose shoes I am not worthy to unloose: **He shall baptize you with the Holy Ghost and with fire:** *(Luke 3:16, emphasis added)*

For John truly baptized with water; **but ye shall be baptized with the Holy Ghost** *not many days hence. (Acts 1:5, emphasis added)*

But ye shall receive power [dunamis], after that the Holy Ghost is come upon you: *and ye shall be witnesses unto Me both in Jerusalem, and in all Judaea, and in Samaria, and unto the uttermost part of the earth. (Acts 1:8, amplification & emphasis added)*

And when the day of Pentecost was fully come, they *were all with one accord in one place. And suddenly there came **a sound from heaven** as of a rushing mighty wind, and it filled all the house where they were sitting. And there appeared unto them **cloven tongues like as of fire,** and it sat upon each of them. And they were all **filled with the Holy Ghost,** and began to **speak with other tongues,** as the Spirit gave them utterance. (Acts 2:1-4, emphasis added)*

According to the Scriptures provided to us by our King, Jesus Christ, and His forerunner John the Baptist and the other witnesses in the Book of Hebrews, here is what happened on the Day of Pentecost, and what should happen in the life of every Believer:

1) The Believers present became heirs of Salvation, made possible by believing in the death and resurrection of Jesus Christ their King. He left permanently to sit at the right hand of God as He ascended back to heaven (Psalm 110:1-2, Acts 1:9-10).

2) Cloven tongues as of fire sat upon each of these Believers. The cloven tongues of fire were individual angels, a flame of fire, a ministering spirit assigned to each one of them as they became an heir of salvation. This also fulfills the promise by John the Baptist that they would be baptized with fire.

3) Each Believer is filled with the Holy Ghost. This is what Jesus meant when He said, "You shall be baptized with the Holy Ghost not many days hence." They were literally submerged and immersed in the Holy Spirit.

4) They each began to speak in other tongues using one of the nine gifts of the Holy Ghost available to every Believer. This is the *dunamis* power that Jesus was talking about when He said: "You shall receive power, after that the Holy Ghost has come upon you." They spoke in tongues immediately after the Holy Ghost came upon them, so this must be the power that Jesus promised they would receive after this event. Simply put, speaking in tongues generates the power of the Holy Ghost (see John 4:10-14, 7:38-39). Peter also later explained that speaking in tongues was also prophesying (Acts 2:16-18). They were simply prophesying the wonderful works of God in a language unknown to the speakers (Acts 2:11).

Fire and Healing

It took me a long time to discover this or to even realize what was happening. I finally realized that the reason my hands would heat up when I would be in the presence of the sick was because the angel assigned to me was ready to minister for me as I was obedient to follow the leading of the Holy Ghost. My hands or sometimes my entire body would heat up because the ministering spirit assigned to me, a flame of fire, was creating the spiritual heat necessary to lay hands on the sick that they might recover. The gifts of healing and the working of miracles, two of the nine gifts of the Holy Spirit were available to manifest the Kingdom of God on earth as it is in heaven.

Your Assigned Angel

One of the best kept secrets of the Bible about angels being assigned to humans is found within the Story of

Moses on Mount Sinai. Most of us are familiar with the movie *The Ten Commandments (1956)* staring Charlton Heston or *The Prince of Egypt* (1998) animated movie. Both of these movies are a great modern day retelling of the original story of Moses found in the book of Exodus. Here is a snapshot of Moses' angelic Sinai experience:

> *Now, Moses kept the flock of Jethro his father in law, the priest of Midian: and he led the flock to the backside of the desert, and came to the mountain of God, even to Horeb. And **the angel of the LORD appeared unto him in a flame of fire out of the midst of a bush:** and he looked, and, behold, the bush burned with fire, and the bush was not consumed. And Moses said, I will now turn aside, and see this great sight, why the bush is not burnt. And when the LORD saw that he turned aside to see, God called unto him out of the midst of the bush, and said, Moses, Moses. And he said, Here am I. And He said, Draw not nigh hither: put off thy shoes from off thy feet, for the place whereon thou standest is holy ground. (Exodus 3:1-5, emphasis added)*

When we see the movies about Moses and his experience on Mount Sinai with the burning bush and how he later delivered the children of Israel from Egypt with a mighty hand, we are left in awe at the signs, wonders and miracles he performed. We love to rehearse the "Let My People Go" command of Moses to Pharaoh as he unleashed signs and plagues from turning his staff to a serpent to finally killing the firstborn of Egypt. Moses, with the help of his brother Aaron, exhibits such power and favor from God as he is transformed into a great deliverer right before our eyes.

One of the great mysteries that is not explicitly mentioned when we read the Exodus account or at all explored when we watch any of the movies is the real purpose the angel of the Lord served in the story. The angel of the Lord is used as a liaison or representative of God as He talks to Moses out of the burning bush (and most of us are satisfied with that simple explanation). But I was very surprised several years ago when reading the book of Acts rendition of this same account. See if you notice the same thing I did, starting in Acts 7:30:

> *And when forty years were expired, there appeared to him in the wilderness of mount Sina **an angel of the Lord in a flame of fire** in a bush. When Moses saw it, he wondered at the sight: and as he drew near to behold it, the voice of the Lord came unto him, Saying, I am the God of thy fathers, the God of Abraham, and the God of Isaac, and the God of Jacob. Then Moses trembled, and durst not behold. Then said the Lord to him, Put off thy shoes from thy feet: for the place where thou standest is holy ground. I have seen, I have seen the affliction of my people which is in Egypt, and I have heard their groaning, and am come down to deliver them. And now come, I will send thee into Egypt. This Moses whom they refused, saying, Who made thee a ruler and a judge? The same did God send to be a ruler and a deliverer **by the hand of the angel which appeared to him in the bush.** He brought them out, after that He had **shewed wonders and signs** in the land of Egypt, and in the Red sea, and in the wilderness forty years. (Acts 7:30-36, emphasis added)*

Did you see what I saw? I always thought Moses met the angel of the Lord on Mount Sinai, received his instructions from the Lord about delivering Israel, and went back to Egypt to command Pharaoh to "Let my people go" by the power of God using signs, wonders and miracles. And that is true! What I did not realize is that Moses did not directly work the signs, wonders and miracles, himself. The wonders and signs were done by the hand of the angel which appeared to him in the bush. I was always under the impression that Moses descended from the mountain and left the angel of the Lord there (or it probably went back to heaven) while he went and delivered the children of Israel from Egypt. It was never brought to my attention that the angel of the Lord followed Moses down from the mountain and worked the wonders and signs we read about "for him." This is consistent with the function of assigned angels we read from the book of Hebrews:

> *Are they not all ministering spirits,* **sent forth to minister for them who shall be heirs of salvation?** *(Hebrews 1:14, emphasis added)*

The fact that the angel of the Lord had the ability to cause the bush to burn without being consumed is also consistent with what we read earlier:

> *And of the angels He saith, Who maketh His angels spirits,* **and His ministers a flame of fire.** *(Hebrews 1:7, emphasis added)*

It's almost hard to believe I never saw that in all the times I previously read the book of Acts.

Angels and the Laying on of Hands

We also see angels at work directly through the laying on of hands. When we study this, it becomes apparent it is not a new doctrine. This is not a vertical truth, but is a normal practice of the Kingdom of God seen horizontally in the Scriptures from Genesis to Revelation. Our ancient patriarch Jacob, known also as Israel, gives us this example:

*And Joseph said unto his father, They are my sons, whom God hath given me in this place. And he said, **Bring them, I pray thee, unto me, and I will bless them.** Now the eyes of Israel were dim for age, so that he could not see. And he brought them near unto him; and he kissed them, and embraced them. And Israel said unto Joseph, I had not thought to see thy face: and, lo, God hath shewed me also thy seed. And Joseph brought them out from between his knees, and he bowed himself with his face to the earth. And Joseph took them both, Ephraim in his right hand toward Israel's left hand, and Manasseh in his left hand toward Israel's right hand, and brought them near unto him. And Israel stretched out his right hand, and laid it upon Ephraim's head, who was the younger, and his left hand upon Manasseh's head, guiding his hands wittingly; for Manasseh was the firstborn. **And he blessed Joseph,** and said, God, before whom my fathers Abraham and Isaac did walk, the God which fed me all my life long unto this day, **the angel which redeemed me from all evil, bless the lads;** and let my name be named on them, and the name of my fathers Abraham and Isaac; and let them grow into a multitude in the midst of the earth. (Genesis 48:9-16, emphasis added)*

Now, we know the rest of the story. Joseph was displeased with his father, Israel, because he put his right hand on the younger instead of the older to give him more of the blessing. However, Israel assures Joseph that though his eyesight may be lacking, that he is not senile, and very much intended to bless the younger before the older. What I do not want us to miss, again, is the fact that Jacob does not directly release the blessing on his life to the next generations. Though Jacob says, "I will bless them," it is the angel of the Lord that was directly commanded to "bless the lads" on Jacob and God's behalf. It is the angel of the Lord, that ministering spirit, that flame of fire, personally assigned to Jacob that releases the blessing "for him."

You see, each of us that are born again Believers in Jesus Christ, Abraham's seed, have an angel of the Lord assigned to us, sent to help us fulfill the will of God for our generation and for our lives. That angel came the day we became heirs of salvation. This benefit is what connects us to the realm of signs, wonders and various miracles from heaven. We are not to pray to our assigned angel (Revelation 22:8-9), but only to our Father who is in heaven (Matthew 6:9). The angel knows to move to assist us when we are operating in the will of God. The Scriptures tell us they move when they hear the Voice of His Word:

> *Bless the LORD, ye His angels, that excel in strength, that do His commandments, hearkening unto the Voice of His Word. Bless ye the LORD, all ye His hosts; ye ministers of His, that do His pleasure. (Psalm 103:20-21)*

Our assignment is to cause His Kingdom, continually, to come on earth as it is in heaven. The angels of the Lord know what it is like in heaven and are tasked to help us bring our Father's will to pass. Because the angels are flames of fire, it is not unusual to feel heat in our hands (through the laying on of hands) or over our entire bodies (a spiritual baptism or covering of spiritual fire), when God's angels (ministering spirits) are around us and ready to act on our behalf.

- Chapter 9 -
Prophetic Healing

Before I share this chapter on prophetic healing, I need to make sure you understand the principle of speaking by NOW Faith and the principle of the prayer of faith (go back to Chapter 6 if you need a refresher). The reason is that healing works prophetically (as do all things in the Kingdom of God). By prophetically, I mean to speak as we are led by the Holy Ghost as He gives revelation (words) directly to someone or something from the Father in heaven.

Receiving this kind of revelation (expressed words) from God is different than the way we receive it from the Scriptures, though they are both the Word of God. What is the difference?

The *logos* word of God:

Generally speaking, the Word of God in the Scriptures – the 66 books of the Bible – are the written Word of God. The written Word of God is the Greek word *logos.* These are the infallible Scriptures that are unchanging and to which nothing can be added (2 Timothy 3:15-16; 2 Peter 1:19-21). This kind of word, because it is written, was given in the past. Because the Word of God is alive (Hebrews 4:12), we can use it for today, but it will not say something new if we open our Bibles tomorrow. The Word of God, because it is unchanging, also refers to God Himself (John 1:1-3) and is manifested in the form of Jesus Christ (John 1:14-18).

The *rhema* word of God:

The second kind of word of God mentioned in the Scriptures is the Greek word *rhema*. A *rhema* word is a right now word from the Father in heaven. Jesus spoke about this kind of word when speaking to His adversary, the devil. He said:

> But He answered and said, It is written, Man shall not live by bread alone, but by every [**rhema**] word that proceedeth out of the mouth of God. (Matthew 4:4, amplification added)

[Note: I am using the phrases "*logos* word" and "*rhema* word" in the same grammatical order that I used "*dunamis* power" earlier in this book. I am aware that I am saying word-word by using these phrases. I agree that it is a redundant phrase and am only using it to specify the kind of word of which I am speaking].

A *rhema* word is an expressed, right now word from God. When we speak this word under the influence of the Holy Ghost, it is a prophetic word. It is a word we receive by revelation from the Father in heaven (Matthew 16:17). Speaking in this way is one of the foundational reasons why Jesus Christ gave His life for us, so we could receive the Holy Ghost (also known as the Spirit of Truth, the Holy Spirit and the Comforter). The Holy Ghost gives us the ability to prophesy, *etc.*

> Howbeit, when He, **the Spirit of truth,** is come, He will guide you into all truth: for He shall not speak of Himself; but whatsoever He shall hear, that shall He speak: **and He**

will shew you things to come. (John 16:13, emphasis added)

But the **Comforter**, *which is* **the Holy Ghost**, *whom the Father will send in My Name,* **He shall teach you all things,** *and bring all things to your remembrance, whatsoever I have said unto you.* (John 14:26, emphasis added)

And it shall come to pass in the last days, saith God, I will pour out of **my Spirit** *upon all flesh: and your sons and your daughters* **shall prophesy,** *and your young men shall see visions, and your old men shall dream dreams: And on My servants and on My handmaidens, I will pour out in those days of My Spirit; and they* **shall prophesy:** (Acts 2:17-18, emphasis added)

But the **manifestation of the Spirit** *is given to every man to profit withal. For to one is given by the Spirit* **the word of wisdom;** *to another the* **word of knowledge** *by the same Spirit; to another* **faith** *by the same Spirit; to another* **the gifts of healing** *by the same Spirit; to another* **the working of miracles;** *to another* **prophecy;** *to another* **discerning of spirits;** *to another* **divers kinds of tongues;** *to another* **the interpretation of tongues**: *but all these worketh that one and the selfsame Spirit, dividing to every man severally as He will.* (1 Corinthians 12:7-11, emphasis added)

The ability to prophesy comes from the Holy Spirit. It is one of His gifts. We are told in 1 Corinthians 14:1 that it is the most important of all the spiritual gifts. That is because all of the Holy Spirit's gifts work prophetically. If you can learn how to hear a word from the Lord in the now, then you can learn how to prophesy. If you can learn how to prophesy, then you can operate in all nine gifts of the Holy Spirit.

Because there are already many good books about prophecy and the prophetic, I will not spend much time to break down the subject here. However, if you are near the beginning of your prophetic journey or just need to be sharpened, I recommend that you read the Personal Prophecy Series by Dr. Bill Hamon. He has already written three very sound volumes on this subject:

- Prophets and Personal Prophecy
- Prophets and the Prophetic Movement
- Prophets, Pitfalls and Principles

I humbly recommend that you start there if you need more help. If you just cannot read three books and need just one book about prophecy, I recommend *God Still Speaks: How to Hear and Receive Revelation from God for Your Family, Church, and Community* by John Eckhardt. Both of these authors offer sound biblical teaching on this subject and will always direct you back to the Scriptures to avoid error.

Prophecy & Healing

Jesus was always healing the sick. He mainly used the gift of faith (a type of prophetic *rhema* word known as the word of faith, Romans 10:8, 17) along with the laying on of hands (through the gifts of healing) to manifest those healings. (Not by coincidence, both gifts are found in 1 Corinthians 12:9.) This is the main method that He taught His disciples, as well. It is the predominant, though not only method we see used by Jesus and His many disciples in the Scriptures. We know this because Jesus spends much time in the NT showing us that faith and healing go together (*e.g.*, Matthew 8:10, 9:22, 15:28; Mark 5:34, 10:52; Luke 8:48, 17:19).

We heal prophetically by releasing a word of faith. A word of faith comes by hearing a *rhema* word from God. The Scriptures tell us this directly:

> *But what saith it?* ***The [rhema] word is nigh thee****, even in thy mouth, and in thy heart: that is,* ***the [rhema] word of faith****, which we preach; (Romans 10:8, amplification & emphasis added)*

> *So then, faith cometh by hearing, and hearing by the [**rhema**] word of God. (Romans 10:17, amplification added)*

This means that someone must complete the activity of hearing from God in the now to speak a word of faith. It is this word of faith that must be spoken prophetically to initiate a healing. Let's look at a previous example of laying on of hands and we will see that it also contains a word of faith:

> *Now, Peter and John went up together into the temple at the hour of prayer, being the ninth hour. And a certain man lame from his mother's womb was carried, whom they laid daily at the gate of the temple which is called Beautiful, to ask alms of them that entered into the temple; who seeing Peter and John about to go into the temple asked an alms. And Peter, fastening his eyes upon him with John, said, Look on us. And he gave heed unto them, expecting to receive something of them.* ***Then Peter said, Silver and gold have I none; but such as I have give I thee: In the Name of Jesus Christ of Nazareth, rise up and walk. And he took him by the right hand, and lifted him up:*** *and immediately his feet and ankle bones received strength. (Acts 3:1-7, emphasis added)*

You see, not only did Peter use the laying on of hands to make physical contact with the lame man to transfer *dunamis* power for healing, he also commanded the man to rise up and walk. This is a word of faith. Peter positioned the lame man, so he would be "expecting to receive something of them" to initiate the healing with a *rhema* word of faith.

Here is another example by Paul:

*And there sat a certain man at Lystra, impotent in his feet, being a cripple from his mother's womb, who never had walked: the same heard Paul speak: who stedfastly beholding him, and perceiving that he had faith to be healed, **said with a loud voice, Stand upright on thy feet.** And he leaped and walked. (Acts 14:8-10, emphasis added)*

Awesome! Again, we see the *rhema* word of faith initiates the healing!

Now, why is it important to know that the word of faith must happen prophetically? I'm glad you asked. The prophetic implies that the words I am going to say do not come from me, the speaker, but from the Holy Ghost. That is the difference. Before I speak a word of faith, I must recognize that it is not a preconceived Word from me or from the Bible. The word of faith is a *rhema* word, and therefore, I am seeking what I will say from the Holy Ghost in that moment. If what I say happens to be a Scripture, then so be it. But I do not have my mind made up about what I will say before going into the healing. In fact, in the last two examples, neither Peter nor Paul proceed until they perceive that the person needing healing, is expecting to receive something from them or has faith to even be healed. It is upon this perception that they are moved by the Holy Spirit to speak a *rhema* word of faith. Notice again, that they speak directly to the person, using the prayer of faith, instead of praying about the sickness or the disease in the person's life. Also, notice that the prayer of faith is released by using a *rhema* word of faith, prophetically, to initiate a healing.

Speaking in Tongues and the Word of Faith

By far, the best way to receive a word of faith is by speaking in tongues. Speaking in tongues is also called "praying in the Spirit" (1 Corinthians 14:2, 14-15, Jude 20). When we pray in the Spirit, it gives us access to the language of the Holy Ghost as well as the promised wisdom and revelation (Ephesians 1:17) from the Father in heaven. Specifically, praying in the Spirit increases our access to the gift of Faith:

> *But ye, beloved, building up yourselves on your most holy faith, praying in the Holy Ghost (Jude 20)*

Speaking in tongues allows us to have the faith necessary to speak to our mountains and command them to be moved. Speaking in tongues allows us to know what to say at the proper time as we are led by the Holy Ghost. The Holy Ghost, through praying in the Spirit, also assists in our healing. I also believe this to be another interpretation of Romans 8:26:

> *Likewise, the Spirit also helpeth our **infirmities:** for we know not what we should pray for as we ought: but the Spirit itself maketh intercession for us with groanings which cannot be uttered. (Romans 8:26, emphasis added)*

This verse tells us that the Holy Spirit intercedes for us to help our infirmities. Many scholars interpret the Greek word ***astheneia*** to mean "weaknesses," meaning: the Holy Spirit intercedes for us, because we are too weak to know what we should pray ourselves. Though I believe this is also true, the Greek word ***astheneia*** can also be translated as meaning sicknesses and diseases. With that understanding, we can deduce that the Holy Ghost increases our faith when we pray in the Spirit, so that we can receive help when we are faced with sickness and disease.

In the next part of this book, we will discuss how Jesus used the power of the *rhema* word to cast out demons in conjunction with healing all manner of sickness and disease. Our King is a total healing Ruler committed to making sure we live life to the full (John 10:10). Walk with me as we explore the wonderful world of healing and deliverance!

The Revelation of Healing

- Part 3 -
Healing & Deliverance

The Revelation of Healing

- Chapter 10 -
What is Deliverance?

Deliverance represents spiritual healing in the Health Care Plan of the Kingdom of God. The word "deliverance" in the NT comes from the Greek word *aphesis*, meaning "release from bondage, darkness or imprisonment." It means forgiveness or pardon of sins and their sentence or penalty. The prophet Isaiah proclaimed the deliverance of Israel:

> *That thou mayest say to the prisoners, Go forth; to them that are in darkness, shew yourselves. (Isaiah 49:9a)*

Deliverance represents exposing the works of the Kingdom of Darkness. To deliver is to set free those that are bound. To deliver is to shine a bright light on that which is hidden in unrighteousness. Deliverance requires that which is in darkness to be brought to the marvelous light (1 Peter 2:9).

The Hebrew and Greek words for "darkness" – *choshek* and *scotia* – both imply the secret place of darkness. They mean the outer realm or prison, to be in outer darkness. This is the state used in the Scriptures to describe Hades (hell) and the underground prison. Darkness simply means the absence of light, where light is a representation of revelation, freedom and prosperity.

Jesus came to bring deliverance to Israel and to the whole world. His first public proclamation from the book of Isaiah is a direct attack on the Kingdom of Darkness:

And there was delivered unto Him the book of the prophet Esaias. And when He had opened the book, He found the place where it was written, The Spirit of the Lord is upon me, because He hath anointed me to preach the gospel to the poor; He hath sent me to heal the brokenhearted, to preach deliverance to the captives, and recovering of sight to the blind, to set at liberty them that are bruised, to preach the acceptable year of the Lord. (Luke 4:17-19)

This first proclamation of Jesus about why He came to the earth is very important to understand. It is very important to accept that Jesus came to heal, set free and deliver! He came to stand against and defeat Satan and his Kingdom of Darkness and Oppression. He came to set the captives and prisoners free who were bound by the law of sin and death. The Bible tells us this was His specific reason for coming:

*The word which God sent unto the children of Israel, preaching peace by Jesus Christ: (He is Lord of all:) That word, I say, ye know, which was published throughout all Judaea, and began from Galilee, after the baptism which John preached; how God anointed Jesus of Nazareth with the Holy Ghost and with power: Who went about doing good, **and healing all that were oppressed of the devil;** for God was with Him. (Acts 10:36-38, emphasis added)*

Jesus was a deliverance minister. He was about the Father's business of setting the captives free. He was about the business of unlocking jail cells. He was about the business of having mercy and removing those things that hinder our lives. He wanted God's people to be free. Jesus was the ultimate pardoner. All the presidents of the United States of America combined have not pardoned more people than Jesus. If you want to hold unforgiveness toward someone, don't look for Jesus to take your side. He would set them free. I might as well say it, "Whom the Son sets free is free indeed!"

Once we understand the previous Scriptures, we can revisit the Cross. We understood from Isaiah 53:4-5 that Jesus ultimately died on the Cross for four main reasons:

1) To heal sickness and disease
2) To heal pains, anxieties and sorrows
3) To forgive our transgressions
4) To forgive our iniquities

We can now expand on #2 (above) and conclude the following:

1) Jesus had a commitment to heal the spiritual and emotional part of man
2) Jesus was committed to healing the broken-hearted and bruised
3) Jesus' power for deliverance came from the Holy Ghost!

These points, though simple, are significant because they reveal that Jesus cares about our broken hearts. Many of us have been broken, abused and battered by bad and broken relationships. We have been held captive by fear, rejection, condemnation, shame, sorrow and bad decisions. Jesus came to mend our broken hearts and set us free from these oppressions of the devil. Jesus' commitment to deliverance proves that He came to heal the inner and outer man. You can be made whole! You can be completely healed!

- Chapter 11 -
Deliverance & Apostolic Power

*A*nd *when He had called unto Him His twelve disciples, He gave them power against unclean spirits, to cast them out, and to heal all manner of sickness and all manner of disease. Now the names of the twelve apostles are these; The first, Simon, who is called Peter, and Andrew his brother; James the son of Zebedee, and John his brother; Philip, and Bartholomew; Thomas, and Matthew the publican; James the son of Alphaeus, and Lebbaeus, whose surname was Thaddaeus; Simon the Canaanite, and Judas Iscariot, who also betrayed Him. (Matthew 10:1-4)*

The apostles of Jesus Christ were those called to wield the power of healing and casting out of devils in the NT. The office of the apostle was new to the Scriptures in the sense that it was not an office we see in the OT (at least by this name, anyway). Clearly, the New Covenant King, Jesus Christ, created this new office to wage war on the unclean spirits that were roaming about the earth as well as the epidemic of sickness and disease on the planet in His day.

The unique thing about the office of the apostle that we never saw before in the Scriptures is that the apostles were specialists in casting out unclean spirits (also known as devils or demons). No other office in the Scriptures is shown as being specialists in this area (*i.e.,* kings, judges, priests, prophets, evangelists, pastors, teachers, *etc.*). The apostles were practitioners in standing against the Kingdom of Darkness and the principalities, powers and rulers of darkness that sustain it (Ephesians 6:12). They were raised up by the Lord Jesus to be experts in the unseen realm whether against Christ's adversary, the devil, or to bring forth the supernatural power of the Kingdom through the Holy Ghost. The apostle's job was to drive out Christ's enemy (the devil) in all his forms and to replace his dark kingdom with the Kingdom of Light. Their assignment was to cause the Kingdom of God to come on earth as it is in heaven.

The apostles were the NT manifestation by Christ of the OT kings. The OT kings of Israel were commissioned to drive out the physical enemies of God (*e.g.,* the descendants of the giants, Anakim, Philistines, *etc.*) out of the Promised Land. They stood against the physical Kingdom of Darkness and were responsible to establish the physical Kingdom of Israel in the earth. The apostles had the same commission but with a spiritual context. They were responsible to drive out the spiritual enemies of God (*i.e.,* demons, principalities, *etc.*) from the Promised Land. They were responsible to establish the spiritual Kingdom of Israel, called the Church, on earth as it is in heaven (Matthew 6:10; Hebrews 12:22-24).

The special gift given by Christ to the apostles that made them unique was the ability to cast out unclean spirits. This was their unique apostolic power! It is difficult to understand the NT without embracing this shift in Kingdom government. Jesus is no longer interested in killing the physical enemies of Israel; that battle was won in the OT. The remaining enemies of Christ are spiritual enemies in the battle against the law of sin and death. These enemies, demons, must also be made the footstool of Christ before the entire war for planet earth can be won (Psalm 110:1-2). [I will write a very extensive book about this one day, but for now I think you are beginning to get the point.]

The apostle's gift, power against unclean spirits, to cast them out, was also coupled with the ability to heal all kinds of sickness and disease. We talked about the necessity of eliminating sickness and disease as it relates to Jesus' death on the cross back in Chapter 2. Sickness and disease are both agents of death. It was necessary for Jesus to defeat these foes to overcome the condemnation the law of sin and death brought upon all mankind. When we understand this concept, we can see clearly that Jesus' death was the final launching pad to allow His new line of kings, called apostles, to wage the final war on sin and death and eliminate his enemy, Satan, forever.

Sickness, Disease & Unclean Spirits

Now that we know that Jesus gave His life to overcome the law of sin and death, and with it, sickness and disease, the next logical question is: "How is the casting out of unclean spirits important to fulfilling this mission?" Excellent question and the answer is simple. Unclean spirits (again, also called demons or devils) are the source of sickness and disease in the lives of many people on this planet. Jesus was well aware of this overarching problem in the earth and came to solve it. Consider again the following Scripture:

The word which God sent unto the children of Israel, preaching peace by Jesus Christ: (He is Lord of all:) That word, I say, ye know, which was published throughout all

Judaea, and began from Galilee, after the baptism which John preached; how God anointed Jesus of Nazareth with the Holy Ghost and with power: Who went about doing good, and healing all that were oppressed of the devil; for God was with Him. (Acts 10:36-38)

Jesus was specifically sent to earth and anointed by God the Father to heal all that were oppressed of the devil. What is interesting to note is that people need healing, because many times, the source is demonic oppression. People are in need of deliverance. This fact is clear by reading several Scriptures. I would like to build my case for casting out unclean spirits, beginning with Matthew's account (which also happens to be the main, though not the only, form of deliverance in which Jesus operated by the power of the Holy Ghost):

*And when Jesus was come into Peter's house, He saw his wife's mother laid, and sick of a fever. And He touched her hand, and the fever left her; and she arose, and ministered unto them. When the even was come, **they brought unto Him many that were possessed with devils: and cast out the spirits with His word, and healed all that were sick**: that it might be fulfilled which was spoken by Esaias the prophet, saying Himself took our infirmities, and bare our sicknesses. (Matthew 8:14-17, emphasis added)*

It is plain to see here and cannot be denied, that a major part of Jesus' healing ministry was the casting out of devils. It is also revealed here again (as we proved back in Chapter 1: The Revelation of Healing) that Jesus gave His life on the cross of Calvary for physical healing. Also proven here is that Jesus gave His life on the cross to guarantee that we could be free from demonic possession of the devil through the deliverance ministry of casting out devils. This too was fulfilled by the prophecy in Isaiah 53:4-5. This is also consistent with Jesus' calling to heal all those oppressed of the devil (Acts 10:38). Demonic possession is obviously a kind of oppression of the devil that Jesus was anointed of the Holy Ghost to cure.

Understanding this doctrine is very important because it helps us to know that being delivered from unclean spirits was purchased for us by Jesus' own blood on the cross. It is a part of the "Package Deal." It also helps us to understand why Jesus cast out demons to bring about physical healing in so many cases of sickness and disease. It is because the unclean spirits were causing the sickness and disease in the life of the person.

I have personally been involved with many cases of praying for people that need healing. I have spent many hours praying in English, speaking in tongues and laying on of hands, trying to get God's people (or one of their relatives) healed of all manner of sickness and disease (*e.g.*, headaches, cancer, diabetes, asthma, back pain, migraines, multiple sclerosis, knee pain, kidney disease, high blood pressure, hearing disorders, ADD, ADHD, depression, narcolepsy, insomnia, glaucoma, upset stomach, irritable bowel syndrome, *etc.*). Often, during these times, the saints and I have prayed with no breakthrough in sight; only to be told by the Holy Spirit that we must first cast out an unclean spirit from the person's life before the sickness or disease can be cured.

There are many more Scriptures that testify to this connection between unclean spirits, sickness and disease:

Heal the sick, cleanse the lepers, raise the dead, cast out devils: freely ye have received, freely give. (Matthew 10:8)

And at even, when the sun did set, they brought unto Him all that were diseased, and them that were possessed with devils. And all the city was gathered together at the door. And He healed many that were sick of divers diseases, and cast out many devils; and suffered not the devils to speak, because they knew Him. (Mark 1:32-34)

And they cast out many devils, and anointed with oil many that were sick, and healed them. (Mark 6:13)

And these signs shall follow them that believe; In My Name shall they cast out devils; they shall speak with new tongues; they shall take up serpents; and if they drink any deadly thing, it shall not hurt them; they shall lay hands on the sick, and they shall recover. (Mark 16:17-18)

Now when the sun was setting, all they that had any sick with divers diseases brought them unto Him; and He laid His hands on every one of them, and healed them. And devils also came out of many, crying out, and saying, Thou art Christ the Son of God. And He rebuking them suffered them not to speak: for they knew that He was Christ. (Luke 4:40-41)

And He said unto them, Go ye, and tell that fox, Behold, I cast out devils, and I do cures to day and to morrow, and the third day I shall be perfected. (Luke 13:32)

Then Philip went down to the city of Samaria, and preached Christ unto them. And the people with one accord gave heed unto those things which Philip spake, hearing and seeing the miracles which he did. For unclean spirits, crying with loud voice, came out of many that were possessed with them: and many taken with palsies, and that were lame, were healed. (Acts 8:5-7)

You see, there are many sicknesses and diseases that are healed automatically when the unclean spirit causing them is expelled.

You see, there are many sicknesses and diseases that are healed automatically when the unclean spirit causing them is expelled.

The Operation of Unclean Spirits

The job of an unclean spirit is to torment and drive a person to do unrighteous things that they would not otherwise do:

*(For He had commanded the unclean spirit to come out of the man. For oftentimes it had caught him: and he was kept bound with chains and in fetters; and he brake the bands, **and was driven of the devil into the wilderness.**) (Luke 8:29, emphasis added)*

Unclean spirits accomplish this by creating a stronghold in the mind of a person so that evil becomes a normal part of their train of thought or imaginations. Unclean spirits enter the body and attack the mind, which is a part of the soul. Because of this basic function of unclean spirits, we have been given apostolic power to dislodge demons, loosen their grip on the life of a person, and cast them out. **Apostolic power is casting out power:**

For though we walk in the flesh, we do not war after the flesh: (for the weapons of our warfare are not carnal, but

*mighty through God to the pulling down of strong holds;)
Casting down imaginations, and every high thing that
exalteth itself against the knowledge of God, and bringing
into captivity every thought to the obedience of Christ;
And having in a readiness to revenge all disobedience,
when your obedience is fulfilled. (2 Corinthians 10:3-6)*

Apostolic power is casting out power.

The word "warfare" used here by Paul is the Greek word
strateia. It means military service and apostolic career
(because the word "apostle" was the name given to naval
ship captains during Jesus day). This Scripture teaches us
that the weapons of our "apostolic attack" are not physical
weapons, but they are spiritual weapons made to overcome
psychological warfare. These spiritual weapons work by
destroying strongholds the enemy has placed in our
imaginations and thoughts. These weapons, which are
apostolic in nature, are tailor-made to arrest evil thoughts
put there by the enemy. These weapons are the gift Jesus
gave the early apostles, so they would have power against
unclean spirits to cast them out. This gift of the Holy Ghost
is none other than the seventh gift of the Spirit called
"discerning of spirits."

The Gift of Discerning of Spirits

Discerning of spirits was the gift Jesus gave the early
apostles, so they would have power against unclean spirits.
The phrase "discerning of spirits" simply means
"understanding of spirits." Jesus and His disciples used the
gift in the NT to "understand" what kind of demonic spirits

were at work in the life of a person, so they could use this information to cast the demon(s) out. Discerning of spirits is another prophetic gift of the Holy Ghost. It works by the same rules as the gift of faith. This means you must speak directly "TO" not "ABOUT" the unclean spirit to cast it out.

Jesus used the gift of discerning of spirits to get understanding on how to cast the demon out of the boy when His disciples could not cast it out:

And one of the multitude answered and said, Master, I have brought unto Thee my son, which hath a dumb spirit; and wheresoever he taketh him, he teareth him: and he foameth, and gnasheth with his teeth, and pineth away: and I spake to thy disciples that they should cast him out; and they could not. He answereth him, and saith, O faithless generation, how long shall I be with you? How long shall I suffer you? Bring him unto Me. And they brought him unto Him: and when he saw Him, straightway the spirit tare him; and he fell on the ground, and wallowed foaming. And He asked his father, How long is it ago since this came unto him? And he said, Of a child. And ofttimes it hath cast him into the fire, and into the waters, to destroy him: but if Thou canst do any thing, have compassion on us, and help us. Jesus said unto him, If thou canst believe, all things are possible to him that believeth. And straightway the father of the child cried out, and said with tears, Lord, I believe; help Thou mine unbelief. When Jesus saw that the people came running together, He rebuked the foul spirit, saying unto him, Thou dumb and deaf spirit, I charge thee, come out of him, and enter no more into him. And the spirit cried, and rent him sore, and came out of him: and he was as one dead; insomuch that many said, He is dead. But Jesus took him by the hand, and lifted him up; and he arose. (Mark 9:17-27)

By the gift of discerning of spirits, Jesus asked the father of the boy how long he had been in this condition. When he learned that the spirit came into the boy when he was a child, He discerned the unclean spirit was a deaf and dumb spirit. Jesus rebuked the demon by name and charged it to come out of the boy. After the spirit came out, Jesus used the laying on of hands to lift the boy by the hand and he was healed completely and arose. He also used His authority to command the unclean spirit not to return. This is the advantage of apostolic power through discerning of spirits. It gives us authority and power to drive the devil out of the land.

Apostles are the Key

One of the greatest assignments of the devil has been the systematic dismantling and elimination of the office of apostle in the Body of Christ, the Church. The apostles were the primary office assigned to stand against the Kingdom of Darkness and thwart the enemy's plans against the world. It makes sense, then, that the enemy would want to specifically eliminate this office so that his plan could prosper unhindered by any real opposition. Just like the OT kings were constantly attacked and seduced by the enemy, so the NT office of apostle has been similarly assaulted. This has occurred so the enemy's forces, demons, can run wild and unchecked on the planet, wreaking havoc worldwide.

There is no other office that has been more aggressively attacked from inside and outside the Church than the apostle. The cessationist view that the office of apostle was meant only for the early Church until the 66 books of the

Bible were canonized is supported nowhere in the Scriptures. However, it has been widely preached in the Church over the last century.

The growth of the Church of Jesus Christ has been greatly hindered by the absence of the apostles. I am not convinced by any Scriptures that God intended for the office of apostle to cease. There are no Scriptures that even remotely make this statement. I believe this office will continue as long as the Church is in existence. I also believe the mass absence of the office of apostle from the Church is the reason why we have not seen many signs, wonders, healings, deliverances and miracles in today's Church. It is because the Church lacks the very office assigned to operate in these gifts.

Thank God, the apostles are returning to the Body of Christ! Jesus is again restoring His Church to her full glory. He is returning for a Holy Ghost filled, demon busting, healing, miracle working, faith walking, loving, merciful, patient and peacemaking bride.

Not Apostles Only

Then, He called His twelve disciples together, and gave them power and authority over all devils, and to cure diseases. And He sent them to preach the Kingdom of God, and to heal the sick. (Luke 9:1-2)

One of the main hindrances in the modern-day Church to walking in apostolic power to cast out demons and bring deliverance is the false teaching that the healing and deliverance ministry was limited to Jesus and the apostles of the early Church. We seem to be primarily aware that Christ called the original 12 apostles (and Paul) to do this work. This error in our teaching is simply not true and is not even hidden in the Scriptures:

> *After these things, **the Lord appointed other seventy also,** and sent them two and two before His face into every city and place, whither He Himself would come. (Luke 10:1, emphasis added)*

> *And **heal the sick** that are therein, and say unto them, the Kingdom of God is come nigh unto you. (Luke 10:9, emphasis added)*

> ***And the seventy returned again** with joy, saying, Lord, **even the devils are subject unto us through Thy Name.** And He said unto them, I beheld Satan as lightning fall from heaven. Behold, I give unto you power to tread on serpents and scorpions, and over all the power of the enemy: and nothing shall by any means hurt you. Notwithstanding, in this rejoice not, that the spirits are subject unto you; but rather rejoice, because your names are written in heaven. (Luke 10:17-20, emphasis added)*

Not only did Jesus appoint the 12 original apostles, but He had over 70 other disciples that healed and operated in deliverance ministry by casting out devils. The Scriptures tell us they were also appointed. You see, Jesus never intended for His healing and deliverance power to be limited to the 12 original apostles.

- Part 4 -
Administering Healing & Deliverance Sessions

The Revelation of Healing

- Chapter 12 -
Healing through Self-Deliverance

Before I involve anyone in a healing or deliverance session, I always try to educate them about self-deliverance, first, if I have the opportunity. There is nothing worse than seeing a person experience freedom by finally being healed, set free and delivered for the first time, only to see them become sick again or tormented by the same demonic stronghold later, because they were never told how to maintain their healing or deliverance. The Bible is clear that it is possible for a person to get delivered from an unclean spirit and for it to return to the same person, causing them to be even worse than they were before:

When the unclean spirit is gone out of a man, he walketh through dry places, seeking rest, and findeth none. Then he saith, I will return into my house from whence I came out; and when he is come, he findeth it empty, swept, and garnished. Then goeth he, and taketh with himself seven other spirits more wicked than himself, and they enter in and dwell there: and the last state of that man is worse than the first. Even so shall it be also unto this wicked generation. (Matthew 12:43-45)

For this reason, I put a lot of effort into helping people understand what they must do to maintain their deliverance. I try to be as frank with them as possible.

One of the main things I counsel people to know is that it is very hard to maintain your deliverance if you are not connected with a very good church that believes in healing and deliverance. It is very difficult to stay delivered from any vice on your own strength without some kind of accountability system. You should seek to become a committed member of a Holy Ghost-filled church that believes in teaching the Gospel of the Kingdom of God in the Name of Jesus Christ.

It takes the power of the Holy Ghost to seriously defeat the power of the enemy. The power of deliverance must be consistently available in any Christian environment to foster healthy growth among God's people. Consider the following story about deliverance:

And from thence He arose, and went into the borders of Tyre and Sidon, and entered into an house, and would have no man know it: but He could not be hid. For a certain woman, whose young daughter had an unclean spirit, heard of Him, and came and fell at His feet: the woman was a Greek, a Syrophenician by nation; and she besought Him that He would cast forth the devil out of her daughter. But Jesus said unto her, Let the children first be filled: for it is not meet to take the children's bread, and to cast it unto the dogs. And she answered and said unto Him, Yes, Lord: yet the dogs under the table eat of the children's crumbs. And He said unto her, For this saying go thy way; the devil is gone out of thy daughter. (Mark 7:24-29)

Most readers of this story are astonished at Jesus' response to the Syrophenician women in this story. We are amazed that Jesus said "No" to her initial request. After all, Jesus is supposed to always be merciful toward everyone. However, a great revelation about deliverance is hidden within Jesus' refusal to cast the unclean spirit out of the woman's daughter. Jesus informs the woman that casting the devil out of a person was "the children's bread" (see, also Matthew 15:21-28).

He explained to the woman that the children (the Israelites that need deliverance) had the right to be filled with bread (the ministry of casting out devils), first. In other words, deliverance is the children's bread. This means that deliverance ministry was not meant for people outside of the family of God before it is administered to those inside His family (the Church).

The fact that the casting out of unclean spirits is called "bread" means that it was meant to be a staple food on the table of God's people that they can consistently and regularly partake whenever they need it, without condemnation. It is supposed to be a normal part of the Christian life. This is also why I continue to counsel people that the best way to maintain their deliverance is to make sure they are plugged into a local church that regularly practices healing and deliverance ministry, according to the Scriptures.

Now to Self-Deliverance

Judge not, that ye be not judged. For with what judgment ye judge, ye shall be judged: and with what measure ye mete, it shall be measured to you again. And why beholdest thou the mote that is in thy brother's eye, but considerest not the beam that is in thine own eye? Or how wilt thou say to thy brother, Let me pull out the mote out of thine eye; and, behold, a beam is in thine own eye? Thou hypocrite, first cast out the beam out of thine own eye; and then shalt thou see clearly to cast out the mote out of thy brother's eye. (Matthew 7:1-5)

There are three principles of self-deliverance I would like to unpack for us here:

1) *Judge not, that ye be not judged. For with what judgment ye judge, ye shall be judged: and with what measure ye mete, it shall be measured to you again.*

   Deliverance cannot occur around judgmental people. Judgmental, unforgiving church folks cannot foster a culture of deliverance. Show me a person that is always pointing out everyone's past mistakes or is constantly questioning why people cannot stop committing the same sin repeatedly, and I will show you someone that has never experienced true deliverance.

   Anyone who has experienced true deliverance knows what it feels like to be in bondage to some vice (e.g., drugs, alcohol, pornography, lying, cheating, gambling, manipulating, jealousy, masturbating, stealing, procrastination, sugar, tardiness, depression, over-eating, chocolate, laziness, fornicating, homosexuality, smoking, partying, gossiping, etc.). They just cannot get free from its grasp no matter how hard they may try.

   A person that has experienced deliverance truly wants to stop doing these things, but they just seem to find themselves driven to do it again, week after week, month after month, year after year. Judge not, unless you are judged, is not suggesting that we should live without accountability from other people. It is just pointing out that when we hold others accountable we should be ready for some accountability to be pointed back our way.

The Scriptures are clear that we are called to judge one another in the Body of Christ (1 Corinthians 6:1-11). This is the natural policing method. We should be prepared to live by the same judgments we release on others. That is the way it should be, anyway!

2) *And why beholdest thou the mote that is in thy brother's eye, but considerest not the beam that is in thine own eye? Or how wilt thou say to thy brother, Let me pull out the mote out of thine eye; and, behold, a beam is in thine own eye?*

This is a simple Scripture. The Williams Brothers said it best, "Sweep around your own front door, before you try to sweep around mine!"

3) *Thou hypocrite, first cast out the beam out of thine own eye; and then shalt thou see clearly to cast out the mote out of thy brother's eye.*

Now we're talking. Here is the really good part. There are two fundamental Kingdom steps to deliverance, here. We are told to first "cast out" the beam from our own eye. Remember that the phrase "cast out" is a term used by Jesus to describe the power He gave the apostles to "cast out" unclean spirits.

Second, we are told we will be able to "see clearly" after we remove the beam from our own eye. Those of you who know the Scriptures know that "seeing" is a term used in the OT to describe prophets and the prophetic gift (see 1 Samuel 9:9).

Here is the summary: the beam represents the largest issues in our lives. If we are diligent to apostolically deal with the largest issues in our lives (cast them out), we will also receive the prophetic ability (to see clearly) to help others receive deliverance from their issues as well. This is a simple concept really. When you get delivered from your own stuff, you will be able to see what it takes to get others delivered from their stuff.

Now, without going too deep, this process of self-deliverance is just following the order of the Kingdom. In the Kingdom of God, the apostolic always comes first and then the prophetic. That is the correct order. Jesus, the architect of the Kingdom of God, knew this and is helping us get delivered decently and in order:

And God hath set some in the Church, first apostles, secondarily prophets, thirdly teachers, after that miracles, then gifts of healings, helps, governments, diversities of tongues. (1 Corinthians 12:28)

And are built upon the foundation of the apostles and prophets, Jesus Christ Himself being the Chief Corner Stone; (Ephesians 2:20)

And He gave some, apostles; and some, prophets; and some, evangelists; and some, pastors and teachers; (Ephesians 4:11)

Okay, I wanted to show you those Scriptures to establish that there is some Kingdom order; first the apostolic, then the prophetic. Jesus is telling us to first apply the apostolic, casting out power we possess on our lives (to remove the beam) and then we will have access to prophetic power to see clearly (to remove the mote) and help someone else.

This Might Hurt a Little Bit

Now the only question is, "What must I do to get delivered and stay delivered from the largest issue in my life? Okay, we're almost there, but we will need a few more Scriptures to make it clear:

*That which we have seen and heard declare we unto you, that ye also may have fellowship with us: and truly our fellowship is with the Father, and with His Son Jesus Christ. And these things write we unto you, that your joy may be full. This then is the message which we have heard of Him, and declare unto you, **that God is light, and in Him is no darkness at all.** If we say that we have fellowship with Him, and walk in darkness, we lie, and do not the truth: but if we walk in the light, as He is in the light, we have fellowship one with another, and the blood of Jesus Christ His Son cleanseth us from all sin. If we say that we have no sin, we deceive ourselves, and the truth is not in us. **If we confess our sins, He is faithful and just to forgive us our sins, and to cleanse us from all unrighteousness.** (1 John 1:3-9, emphasis added)*

So, we talked about this before. The Hebrew and Greek words for darkness, **choshek** and **scotia,** respectively, both mean the secret place of darkness. They mean the outer realm or prison, to be in outer darkness. Darkness represents that which is hidden in our lives. It represents those things that have taken place in our lives that we would rather no one else ever see. We desire for it to remain covered. We push it to the back room, deep down in the basement. Here, Paul informs us that God is light, and in Him is no darkness at all.

In our old home, we had a junk room. It actually was supposed to be our office or den. Whenever we would have visitors on short notice, we would begin vigorously cleaning up our home. It would happen that anything for which we could not find a permanent home while cleaning would just get tossed in the junk room. That room allowed our home to appear completely clean, while there was a hidden place on the inside that reflected all the stuff we did not want anyone to see.

Whenever a visitor would try to open the door to that room we would quickly stop them, not wanting them to discover the mess on the inside. We would close the door, turn off the light and hide the mess in outer darkness. Instead of actually cleaning out the room, because of our busy lives, we would be resolved to clean the room later. But, the more we put off addressing the darkness within that room, it seemed to accumulate more junk over time. This made it even harder to bring ourselves to open that door, turn on the light and address the issue within.

This is also how many of us live our lives as Christians. We look good on the outside, but on the inside, we are suffering, suffocating and tormented, because of the dark rooms in our spiritual life. Deep down, we want to address the issues of sin in our life, but the devil convinces us that no one would understand if we ever shared our darkest secrets openly with another person. This lie from the devil inevitably causes a stronghold in our mind that keeps us in bondage and causes us to feel condemned, ashamed and separated from God. It causes us to hide our secrets with our very life, never to come to the light.

Deliverance represents exposing the works of the Kingdom of Darkness. To deliver is to set free those that are bound. To deliver is to shine a bright light on that which is hidden in unrighteousness. Deliverance requires that which is in darkness to be brought to the marvelous light (1 Peter 2:9). Because of this, the Scriptures tell us how to bring our lives out of darkness into the light, so we can receive deliverance. It tells us:

If we confess our sins, He is faithful and just to forgive us our sins, and to cleanse us from all unrighteousness. (1 John 1:9)

Every Christian's Problem with Deliverance

Anyone that has been a Christian for a while knows this basic Bible principle. I learned it in Sunday school as a child, and it is quite simple really:

Whenever you sin, you need to take some time at some point every day and ask God for forgiveness.

I learned to do this based on 1 John 1:9. I was taught to get all my sins out of the way before God, and He would cleanse me of my sins and make me whole again. However, after many years of doing this (and most of you Christians know what I'm saying), I discovered that confessing my sins before the Father in heaven did not eliminate these sins from my life. In fact, I found myself in a vicious cycle of sinning and confessing, sinning and confessing, sinning and confessing – repeatedly. I found myself in bondage to the same habitual sins with no relief in sight. I began to wonder why this Scripture was failing – why I was not getting cleansed from all unrighteousness.

One day, the Lord revealed a great principle concerning the sin-confession process in my life that brought me great deliverance. He revealed to me that it is very difficult to confess your sins to someone who was already present when you committed the sin. It is difficult to confess a secret crime to the person who was there to witness it when it was committed. And this is the problem with confessing our sins to God the Father over and over again. Because, as a Christian, we know that God is omnipresent, meaning He is everywhere and can see everything. It becomes difficult to become completely healed if we confess our sins to Him as if He did not see us commit the crime. In other words, a true confession can only occur when it is spoken to someone who was not present when the transgression was committed.

As Christians, this concept becomes a stronghold for us. The truth is: we are in the bad habit of committing sins repeatedly with the full knowledge that God can see us when we commit them. Because of this fact, it is difficult to have a true confession of our sins, the longer we are saved. It is not much of a confession if the person already knows what you have done.

Technically speaking, if you read 1 John 1:9, the Scripture does not tell us to confess our sins to God. In fact, it does not tell us exactly to whom we should confess our sins. We will need to study another Scripture to discover the life changing answer to that question: "To whom should we confess our sins?"

Is any sick among you? Let him call for the elders of the church; and let them pray over him, anointing him with oil in the Name of the Lord: and the prayer of faith shall save the sick, and the Lord shall raise him up; and if he have committed sins, they shall be forgiven him. **Confess your faults one to another, and pray one for another, that ye may be healed.** *The effectual fervent prayer of a righteous man availeth much. (James 5:14-16, emphasis added)*

Did you just see that? We are not told to confess our sins to God the Father. We are instructed to **confess our faults to one another.** [I told you this would hurt a little bit!] The Scriptures promise, if we are willing to do this, we will be **HEALED.**

Now, I know what you are thinking. You are thinking, "Larry, are you telling me that I need to confess my deepest, darkest secret to someone else, and this will bring me deliverance?" And the answer is a resounding, YES! This is called self-deliverance. It is self-deliverance because it is initiated by you and not someone else.

So, what is the purpose of confessing your sins to another person? Simply put, it exposes and sheds light on the darkness in our lives. When we uncover the hidden sins and thoughts in our lives it brings us into the light and allows us to fully fellowship with God again. Remember, God is light, and in Him is no darkness at all. Hidden sin is the #1 reason why most Christians are not free to worship and serve God fully. These sins cause us to feel condemned, judged, ashamed, rejected, unworthy and unfit to worship our God. Sin causes us to feel dirty when in the presence of a Holy God.

I have been in many Church praise and worship services with the Saints and have witnessed people unable to lift their hands fully before God (I call this alligator arm worship), because they do not feel worthy or clean enough to let themselves go and be spiritually naked before the King. Their conscience will not allow them to be fully transparent before God. They feel like hypocrites in the presence of the Master.

The devil hides in the darkness in our lives. His Kingdom thrives in darkness. In fact, darkness is the exact hiding place of unclean spirits. When an unclean spirit comes into a person's life, it makes its home in the place where they are facilitating unclean thoughts and secret habits that have gone unconfessed. A demon's job is to find a dark place where it can create a stronghold in your life and convince you that you should never, under any circumstances, reveal this dark place to any other person. When a demon has convinced you to do this, it believes it has won the battle and knows that you cannot get real deliverance.

Getting Delivered Correctly

Still here? Let's talk about the elephant in the room. Should you confess your deepest darkest issues or secrets (the beam in your eye) to just anyone in order to get delivered? The answer is a resounding, NO! That would be unwise. Let's go back to the Scripture:

Is any sick among you? **Let him call for the elders of the church**; *and let them pray over him, anointing him with oil in the Name of the Lord: and the prayer of faith shall save the sick, and the Lord shall raise him up; and if he have committed sins, they shall be forgiven him.*

Confess your faults one to another, and pray one for another, that ye may be healed. The effectual fervent prayer of a righteous man availeth much. (James 5:14-16, emphasis added)

Who are the elders of the church? The elders of the church are non-judgmental people who have fruit in their lives that is evidence they are living according to the Word of God (or at least are making a great attempt to do so). Elders are not perfect people. They are people who most likely have been through some things and have experienced deliverance themselves. Because of this, an elder will also know what it will take to maintain your deliverance. The elders are leaders in the church that rule their own households well (see 1 Timothy chapter 3). These are the kinds of people we are encouraged to call when we need healing and forgiveness of sins.

Now, let me be clear here. I am not talking about a Catholic confessional booth where you are confessing to someone you do not know, you cannot see, and who cannot see you. I am talking about setting aside time to meet with someone face to face where you can get proper counseling about your problem and the correct kind of prayer so you can be healed. Are you still here?

Furthermore, when choosing an elder, I am not talking about someone that just has a church title. Unfortunately, not every church leader can be trusted with your information. You should pray and ask God to whom you should confess your sins. It is good to find a non-gossiping church leader that is trained in deliverance.

I am also not teaching that you can no longer confess your sins to God the Father. There are certainly other Scriptures in the Bible that support confessing your sins to

God (Psalm 51:1-4). He will certainly let you know when you have offended Him.

But let me help you a bit further. (You should put your seatbelt on for this one!) Quite often, the person to whom you should confess your sins for the most deliverance is the person to whom you would least want to confess your sins. For example, wives, quite often your husband is the best candidate for your sin confession. Husbands, quite often your wife is the best candidate to confess your sins. Why? Because your spouse will cause you to be the most transparent about your sin(s).

This is true, especially if the sin you have committed is against your spouse. In fact, it is a good practice to confess your sin(s) to the person or persons against whom you have sinned; this will bring you the most deliverance. It will cause the most darkness to come to the light. This exercise will cause you to deal with your own pride and self-righteousness. It will cause the spirit of humility to come upon you. This will uncover the darkness in your life and allow you to walk in freedom, free from the torment of the devil. He will have nowhere to hide once your sins are confessed.

If you find that you cannot stop sinning because there is an unclean spirit oppressing your life, then of course, the elders of the church will be needed to help rid you of the demon and bring about your healing.

Thank you for sticking with me! I hope you are receiving much revelation concerning healing and deliverance. Let's go on to the next chapter to discover how to identify unclean spirits.

- Chapter 13 -
Uncovering Unclean Spirits

From where do demons come? This is the obvious question. Good thing you are reading this book (and I actually have a clue about the answer)!

Before I go there... I will not unfold to you everything about the origin of demons in this chapter. I would need to write another book to cover that subject (and I probably will). Right now, I am only concerned with getting you healed and delivered using this book. I want to give just enough Biblical evidence, so you will know one thing after reading this book: if you have an unclean spirit, you will know what it is and how to get rid of it - forever. Besides, there are already other books on this subject, and I am not attempting to rewrite them here. If I had to recommend a good book on this subject, I would recommend The Serpent's Seed: An Account of the Nephilim by Joel H. Emerson. If you are just beginning on your journey in the subject of deliverance, I recommend reading They Shall Expel Demons by Derek Prince.

That said, let's get right to it (all of you KAC saints know what this means)!

First, we do not read much about unclean spirits in the OT. What we are introduced to in the OT is the concept of the unclean through the Law of Moses.

And that ye may put difference between holy and unholy, and between unclean and clean; and that ye may teach the children of Israel all the statutes which the LORD hath spoken unto them by the hand of Moses. (Leviticus 10:10-11)

There were many things both living and inanimate that could cause one to become unclean, defiled or polluted before the LORD under the Law. To be unclean was to be unholy in the presence of a Holy God. His Name is Holy (Isaiah 57:15, Matthew 6:9).

We are first introduced directly to the phrase "unclean spirit" by the OT prophet, Zechariah. Zechariah prophesied concerning the Messiah, Christ Jesus:

*In that day, there shall be a fountain opened to the house of David and to the inhabitants of Jerusalem for sin and for uncleanness. And it shall come to pass in that day, saith the LORD of hosts, that I will cut off the names of the idols out of the land, and they shall no more be remembered: and also I will cause the prophets and **the unclean spirit** to pass out of the land. (Zechariah 13:1-2, emphasis added)*

Zechariah foresaw that the coming of Christ and His Kingdom would rid the Jews from sin and unclean spirits (the source of the unclean) by the power of the Cross. This prophecy was a fulfillment of the works of the Law through Christ the Messiah. And, of course, we have seen through several Scriptures already, that this is exactly what Jesus did when He showed up on the scene in the NT Gospels of Matthew, Mark, Luke and John:

And there was in their synagogue a man with an unclean spirit; and he cried out, Saying, Let us alone; what have we to do with Thee, Thou Jesus of Nazareth? Art Thou come to destroy us? I know Thee who Thou art, the Holy One of God. And Jesus rebuked him, saying, Hold thy peace, and come out of him. And when the unclean spirit had torn him, and cried with a loud voice, he came out of him. **And they were all amazed, insomuch that they questioned among themselves, saying, What thing is this? What new doctrine is this? For with authority, commandeth He even the unclean spirits, and they do obey Him.** *And immediately His fame spread abroad throughout all the region round about Galilee." (Mark 1:23-28, emphasis added)*

Jesus shifted our attention to the realm of darkness as He confronted the devil openly. Even the Jews recognized the casting out of unclean spirits to be a new doctrine. They had never seen, heard or read of this new ministry in the OT Scriptures. They were aware that unclean spirits existed, but did not have revelation or power to identify or cast them out.

So, the natural question is: from where do unclean spirits come? Here goes:

1) Unclean Spirits are thought to be the exiled spirits of the giants (Nephilim) that lost their bodies during the flood of Noah (Genesis 6:1-7).
2) The word "giants" used here is the Hebrew word **Nphiyl.** This word comes from the root word **naphal,** meaning "fallen" or "cast down."
3) These giants were the offspring of the fallen angels with earthly women (Genesis 6:4, Jude 6-7). They

created a hybrid, unlawful race of super-humans upon the earth (*e.g.*, Goliath).

4) These fallen giants caused the thoughts of mankind to be evil continually (Genesis 6:5) through their sins of rebellion and fornication.

5) When this race of super-humans was wiped out by the flood of Noah, the remaining spirit beings had no immediate lawful eternal destination in heaven (Ecclesiastes 12:7) and were left to roam the earth, looking for new bodies (Matthew 10:28, 12:43-45), thus creating unclean (or impure) spirits. These are spirits that inhabit a body that is not their original host, a kind of parasite.

See, that was quick and easy! No more explanation needed, right? I wish it were that simple.

We continue to see the giants again after the flood of Noah. There are a couple explanations for this:

1) Angels continued to come to earth after the flood and commit the same sin with human women. Perhaps, people were accustomed to this kind of angelic behavior after the flood as well (see Genesis chapter 19), thus creating more giants.

2) One of the sons of Noah, either Japheth or Ham, had some giant DNA in their bloodline. God ultimately chose Shem's pure human bloodline to produce the Messiah through Abraham (so it would not have been that one). One of their bloodlines, either Japheth or Ham, continued to produce giants.

Both schools of thought are Biblically plausible. We could pursue one or both of them. At the end of the day (no matter which one you choose), the OT is mainly about how God is fulfilling His promise to defeat Satan:

> *And the LORD God said unto the serpent, Because thou hast done this, thou art cursed above all cattle, and above every beast of the field; upon thy belly shalt thou go, and dust shalt thou eat all the days of thy life: and I will put enmity between thee and the woman, and between thy seed and her seed; it shall bruise thy head, and thou shalt bruise his heel. (Genesis 3:14-15)*

Satan's seed was planted by making a race of unlawful, hybrid, angel-humans called giants. These giants are the subject of many OT stories (*e.g.*, David and Goliath) and are the thorn in the side of the children of Israel for most of the OT.

When you understand this, the story of the Bible is quite simple. The OT is about purging the earth of all the races of humans that have giant DNA. It was mainly the job of the OT Kings to fulfill this mission (though some judges, prophets and priests got involved as well). King David is lifted up as the main king that fulfilled this mission among many (1 Samuel 18:7). The NT is about purging the earth of the oppression of the devil caused by the spirits of the defeated giants of the OT called unclean spirits. The apostles, as I explained before, are the new covenant kings (along with prophets, evangelists and pastor-teachers) responsible to complete this mission while leading the Church.

Unclean Spirits Identified

Again, unclean spirits are the result of the extermination of the race of giants from this planet. The giants caused the thoughts of men to be evil continually:

*There were giants in the earth in those days; and also after that, when the sons of God came in unto the daughters of men, and they bare children to them, the same became mighty men which were of old, men of renown. And God saw that the wickedness of man was great in the earth, and that **every imagination of the thoughts of his heart was only evil continually.** (Genesis 6:4-5, emphasis added)*

The book of Jude in the NT gives us more detail about this encounter:

And the angels which kept not their first estate, but left their own habitation, *He hath reserved in everlasting chains under darkness unto the judgment of the great day. Even as Sodom and Gomorrha, and the cities about them in like manner, **giving themselves over to fornication, and going after strange flesh,** are set forth for an example, suffering the vengeance of eternal fire. (Jude 1:6-7, emphasis added)*

Jude confirms for us that the angels went after strange flesh (by conceiving with human women that were not a part of the species of angels). This is just another kind of fornication. It was fornication because two different species were procreating (leaving their own habitation) outside of the natural plan of God. Jude gives us further insight into this drama by referring to Enoch, another prophet:

And Enoch also, the seventh from Adam, prophesied of these, saying, Behold, the Lord cometh with ten thousands of His saints, to execute judgment upon all, and to convince all that are ungodly among them of all their ungodly deeds which they have ungodly committed, and of all their hard speeches which ungodly sinners have spoken against Him. (Jude 1:14-15)

What is most interesting is the fact that this passage is taken from the extra-Biblical Book of Enoch (outside of the 66 Books of the Bible), chapter 2. Jude, the brother of Jesus, by referencing this book, gives us permission to investigate its contents further. The Book of Enoch also tells the story of the fallen angels and the giants. It tells us specifically where unclean spirits originate:

> *Now the giants, who have been born of spirit and of flesh, shall be called upon earth evil spirits, and on earth shall be their habitation.* **Evil spirits shall proceed from their flesh, because they were created from above; from the holy Watchers was their beginning and primary foundation. Evil spirits shall they be upon earth, and the spirits of the wicked shall they be called.** *The habitation of the spirits of heaven shall be in heaven; but upon earth shall be the habitation of terrestrial spirits, who are born on earth. The spirits of the giants shall be like clouds,* **which shall oppress, corrupt, fall, content, and bruise upon earth.** *(Enoch 15:8-9, emphasis added)*

The Watchers are Fallen Angels

Even without the Book of Enoch, we have plenty of Scriptures to connect the dots. Unclean spirits were created from the works of the flesh between angels and human women. The result of this sin was that "every imagination of the thoughts of man's heart was evil continually." Therefore, unclean spirits represent the works of the flesh from which they were conceived. The works of the flesh are easy to identify in the Scriptures:

> *Now the works of the flesh are manifest, which are these: adultery, fornication, uncleanness, lasciviousness, Idolatry, witchcraft, hatred, variance, emulations, wrath, strife, seditions, heresies, envyings, murders,*

*drunkenness, revellings, **and such like:** of the which I tell you before, as I have also told you in time past, that they which do such things shall not inherit the kingdom of God. (Galatians 5:19-21, emphasis added)*

Therefore, we cast out unclean spirits of adultery, fornication, witchcraft, murder, *etc.* and any other spirits ("and such like") that would be grouped with these works of the flesh. This is just one list of the works of the flesh. There are other works ("and such like") not named here. Jesus cast out a "dumb and deaf" spirit from a man's son (Mark 9:17-27). Unclean spirits can also travel in groups of different spirits, controlled by a chief spirit. Jesus identified a Legion of spirits like this and cast all of them out at once (Mark 5:9, Luke 8:30).

It is no coincidence that the weapons of our warfare are for the casting down of imaginations (thoughts) that are against the knowledge of God (2 Corinthians 10:3-5). Demons work to cause "every imagination of the thoughts of a heart to be evil continually." They work to drive a person into adultery, murder, hatred, strife, condemnation, shame, fornication, unforgiveness, procrastination, rejection, jealousy, *etc.* Demons' names are associated with the behavior they are trying to perpetuate. They work to create strongholds in a person's thought life in one or many of these areas. You become what you think in your heart (Proverbs 23:7). We are told to put on the helmet of salvation to protect the mind (Ephesians 6:17). We are taught to guard our hearts (Proverbs 4:23). Our hearts possess the issues of our lives. We now know that deliverance from unclean spirits was purchased with salvation on the cross (Isaiah 53:4-5, Matthew 8:16-17). Our deliverance was purchased and secured by the body and blood of Jesus Christ, the King. Deliverance is the children's bread.

Now that we know from where unclean spirits come and how to identify their nature and names, let's shed some light on how to cast them out in the next chapter: Administering the Prayer of Faith for Healing & Deliverance.

- Chapter 14 -
Administering the Prayer of Faith for Healing & Deliverance

If you have skipped to this chapter I would like to encourage you to go back and read the previous 13 chapters. There is much we have messed up in the world and in the Church by trying to execute a short-cut or a get-rich-quick scheme without the proper context and counsel to go alongside the truth. That said, please at least skim the earlier chapters. They are the building blocks upon which the methods in these later chapters are built. Christ desires to build His Church.

Let's continue:

Is any sick among you? Let him call for the elders of the church; **and let them pray over him, anointing him with oil in the Name of the Lord: And the prayer of faith shall save the sick, and the Lord shall raise him up; and if he have committed sins, they shall be forgiven him. Confess your faults one to another, and pray one for another, that ye may be healed.** *The effectual fervent prayer of a righteous man availeth much.* (James 5:14-16, emphasis added)

Okay, here you are sitting before one of the elders of your church, confessing your sins (or perhaps you are the elder). What should happen next? The Scriptures say that the elder should pray over you while anointing you with oil in the Name of the Lord. His Name is Jesus!

STOP! Here is where we usually fail in the healing and deliverance process. At this moment, a church leader will begin praying over you ABOUT the sins you have confessed or praying ABOUT the sickness and disease that is in your life. And there is nothing wrong with praying ABOUT these things, if you know that this is NOT the kind of prayer called for in this Scripture. This Scripture calls for the prayer of faith to be used. And ahaaaaaaaaaaaaaaaaah, we already learned about the prayer of faith back in Chapter 6: Healing by NOW Faith! At this time, you are not looking for anyone to pray ABOUT your sins, sickness or disease. You are looking for someone to speak directly TO your sins, sickness or disease OR any unclean spirit that may be in your life that may be the source of the real problem. Your expectation is that they will pray over you prophetically by using a *rhema* word of faith and speak directly TO you and any issues that may be revealed to them as they are led by the Holy Ghost.

If we put our knowledge from the previous chapters together, we can safely get delivered by following a few steps.

Here are the simple steps to the prayer of faith for deliverance:

1) We ask the person if we have permission to lay hands on them and anoint them with oil. With an affirmative response, place some anointing oil on

their forehead and declare that the peace of God will guard their heart and mind (Philippians 4:6-7).

2) We speak in tongues to give us *dunamis* Power (Chapters 8 & 9).

3) We ask the Holy Ghost to reveal to us what unclean spirits are at work to cause sin in the life of the person using the gift of discerning of spirits (Chapters 9 & 13). [Note: It is sometimes useful to write these down on a dry erase board if there is one available in the room, but a piece of paper will do].

4) Using the gift of discerning of spirits, we call out the unclean spirits by the names we receive from the Holy Ghost (*e.g.,* spirits of fornication, anger, death, fear, rejection, *etc.*) and command them to come out in Jesus' Name:

5) We en-vision the oppressed delivered (Proverbs 23:7; Luke 6:45; Acts 2:17).

6) We speak prophetically by a *rhema* word of faith as the Spirit gives us utterance (Chapter 9).

7) Ask the person to breathe out as the unclean spirits are called out. The word spirit is the Greek word *pneuma.* The word *pneuma* (like in the word pneumonia) is also translated to mean breath or spirit. Because of this, unclean spirits are commonly breath-associated. Asking the person to breathe out simply speeds up expelling the unclean spirit.

8) We use the laying on of hands to transfer the *dunamis* (power) from our body to the person needing the healing and deliverance to drive out the unclean spirit(s). Lay your hand directly on the top of the person's head. You may also use one of their shoulders or upper back, but the head works best.

[WARNING: Under no circumstances should anyone be touched in any private, sensitive area or genitals. A man should lay hands on a woman only with the assistance of another woman of God in ministry. A woman should only lay hands on a man with the assistance of another man of God. I do not mean to be legalistic, but much harm has been done in the Body of Christ because of the lack of wise precautionary measures.]

Remember a few simple Kingdom rules:

1) We speak to unclean spirits and command them to come out. We are to cast them out ONLY (Matthew 10:1). We are not to speak to them for any other purpose.
2) We have been given authority to cast them out (Matthew 10:8; John 1:12; Luke 10:19-20; Mark 16:17-18).
3) We have the gift of discerning of spirits to cast out unclean spirits (1 Corinthians 12:10).

Similarly, here are the simple steps for the prayer of faith for healing:

1) We ask the person if we have permission to lay hands on them and anoint them with oil. With an affirmative response, place some anointing oil on their forehead and declare that the peace of God will guard their heart and mind (Philippians 4:6-7).
2) We speak in tongues to give us *dunamis* Power (Chapters 8 & 9).
3) We ask the Holy Ghost to reveal to us what sicknesses and diseases are at work in the life of the person using the gifts of healings.

4) We ask God to manifest His angels, the flames of fire, a cloven tongue resting upon us. We wait for our hands (or entire body) to heat up as a sign that God is with us. As we see a vision of or from what the person needs healing, we should wait for our hands to heat up with the fire of God.

5) We are to speak directly to the person and declare them healed by a *rhema* word of faith to be healed in Jesus' Name (Chapter 9).

6) We use the laying on of hands to transfer the *dunamis* (power) from our body to the person needing the healing and deliverance to drive out the unclean spirit(s). Lay your hand directly on the top of the person's head. You may also use one of their shoulders or upper back, but the head works best.

[WARNING: Under no circumstances should anyone be touched in any private, sensitive area or genitals. A man should lay hands on a woman only with the assistance of another woman of God in ministry. A woman should only lay hands on a man with the assistance of another man of God. I do not mean to be legalistic, but much harm has been done in the Body of Christ because of the lack of wise precautionary measures.]

I have divided the steps for healing and deliverance into two separate prayers of faith. Of course, as you become disciplined to execute these steps, you will be able to combine the prayers into one activity. Because healing and deliverance work together, you will learn to perform them at the same time.

These steps are not meant to be a legalistic roadmap for the healing and deliverance ministry and should be performed along with a lifestyle of prayer and fasting. (I will cover this in Chapter 16: Preparing for Healing and Deliverance Ministry.)

Because I am apostolic, I believe in detailed diagrams, strategies and roadmaps. I believe things should be done decently and in order (or in as much order as possible). I also believe in creating reproducible processes, so we do not need to start from scratch every time we do something for Jesus. Let's look together in the next chapter at how to put together prophetic healing teams.

- Chapter 15 -
Prophetic Healing Teams

Jesus believed in sending His disciples out in teams. He specifically sent them out two-by-two. I also believe in team ministry. Team ministry cuts down on the super saint complex in which one person has all of the anointing and it is not distributed to anyone else. There are several examples in the Scriptures of the NT model where signs, wonders, miracles, healings and deliverances take place when the apostles and other disciples of Christ operate in teams of two or more. It is this simple Biblical model I would like to popularize and propagate to this generation and beyond.

Here is the prophetic healing teams model:

1) Assemble a team of two or three born-again Believers (preferably church elders) that know how to speak in tongues in prayer. (Note: More Believers can be in the room to Intercede in prayer, but the core team of elders/Believers should not exceed three, see Diagram 15-1).

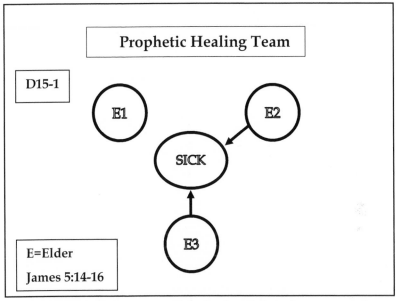

2) Begin praying together in the Spirit (in tongues) to bring about the manifestation of the Holy Ghost in your midst (Matthew 18:18-20; Acts 2:8; see The Manifestation of the Spirit section).

3) As you are praying in the Spirit together, expect God to manifest the greater gifts among you (*e.g.*, prophecy, miracles and healing; see The Greater Gifts section).

4) As team members receive the manifestation of the Spirit individually for the greater gifts, they must immediately notify the rest of the team by a verbal confirmation (*i.e.*, "I have the gift of healing," "I hear the Lord saying," *etc.*; see the Verbal Confirmation section):

   a. What you are seeking first is to see on whom the Spirit distributes the gifts of working of miracles and healings. The team members should look to feel tongues of fire sitting upon them for verification that the angel of the Lord is present to serve with signs, wonders, and diverse miracles. (Note: Commonly a Believer's hands or entire body will heat up when the angel of the Lord and/or the gifts of healing are present.)

   b. Simultaneously, we are looking for the remaining Members to receive a prophetic word (including a word of wisdom, word of knowledge or discerning of spirits).

5) The elders that manifest the gifts of the working of miracles and healing (the healing elders: E1, E2 or E3) should "say so" and immediately begin laying of hands on "the sick" while continuing to pray in the Spirit. The healing elders should keep physical contact until they feel all the virtue within them transfer to "the sick." You will know that virtue (*dunamis* power) has completely gone out of you when your hands go cold and there is no more heat.

6) The rest of the elders (the speaking elders: E1, E2 or E3) should now release the other gifts the Spirit is manifesting to speak the prayer of faith prophetically (see The Prayer of Faith Defined sections).

7) The healing elders (E1, E2 or E3) must verbally notify the group as they feel the virtue (power) of the Holy Ghost flowing out of their hands by saying something like "There it is" or "I feel it flowing out." (Note: the purpose of this verbal notification is to encourage the team and the "the sick" the healing is "effectually" working).

8) All loosing and binding should be done by the authority of the Name of Jesus (see the Binding and Loosing section). This should primarily be done through the gift of discerning of spirits. Any demon spirits should only be bound and cast out! Command the unclean spirits not to return. Remember to ask "the sick" to breathe out as any unclean spirit is called out (as we discussed in the previous chapter).

9) When the team feels there is a pause in the Holy Spirit's flow, the lead elder (E1) should reset the team (going back to step #2) or stop the healing session. (NOTE: The distribution of the gifts by the Holy Ghost may change every time the team is reset. Learn to work together dynamically, in love, without pride.) Also, if possible, E1 should always be an apostle or the most apostolic person. Allow this person to lead and direct the group or presbytery.

10) End with a sealing and closing prayer in Jesus' Name!!!

The Manifestation of the Spirit

- *1 Corinthians 12:7 But the manifestation of the Spirit is given to every man to profit withal.*
- *1 Corinthians 12:11 But all these worketh that one and the selfsame Spirit, dividing to every man severally as He will.*
- *1 Corinthians 12:31 But covet earnestly the best gifts: and yet shew I unto you a more excellent way.*

<u>There are nine gifts of the Holy Spirit listed in 1 Corinthians 12:8-10:</u>

1) The word of wisdom
2) The word of knowledge
3) Faith
4) The gifts of healing
5) The working (*energema*) of miracles (*dunamis*)
6) Prophecy
7) Discerning of spirits
8) Divers kinds of tongues
9) The interpretation of tongues

These are not the only gifts governed by the Holy Ghost in the Scriptures, but they are the only gifts available to every Believer. These are the same gifts Jesus and His more than 70 disciples had available to them. Without these gifts, it would not have been possible for Jesus to send them out two-by-two with an expectation that they could heal the sick, raise the dead, cast out demons and freely give of the Kingdom of God.

We often hear that these gifts are only given "as the Spirit wills." What is meant when people say this is that the Holy Ghost is NOT willing to give all nine gifts to any one person. I do not agree with this teaching. I do not see anywhere in the Scriptures that the disciples commissioned by Christ had any such limitation. There is no Biblical precedent for this teaching by example in the Scriptures. There is no record of any disciple being unable to heal because he only had the gifts of the word of wisdom and the word of knowledge, causing the need for him to find another disciple with the gifts of healing. There is no record of any disciple unable to prophesy because they only had the gifts of faith, diverse kinds of tongues, and discerning of spirits. There is no such story in the Scriptures, because this way of thinking is not a realistic issue. This is not what is meant by "as the Spirit wills." No, "as the Spirit wills" means that the Holy Ghost will release the nine gifts that are within every Believer, as they are needed, one by one, to bring forth total victory as each situation arises. The Holy Ghost comes forth to bring freedom and liberty concerning spiritual things, not to restrict them (2 Corinthians 3:17).

The nine gifts are the manifestation of the Holy Spirit. This means the manifestations belong to Him and not us. The issue is whether or not a person has the Holy Ghost. This is the only issue. If you have the Holy Ghost, then you have all nine gifts within you. If you do not have the Holy Ghost then you have zero gifts within you. There is no need to believe you have two, three, four or five gifts. You have all nine gifts of the Holy Spirit within you if you are a born-again Believer of Jesus Christ.

Prophetic Order

- *1 Corinthians 14:29 Let the prophets speak two or three and let the others judge.*
- *1 Corinthians 14:30 If any thing be revealed to another that sitteth by, let the first hold his peace.*
- *1 Corinthians 14:31 For ye may all prophesy one by one, that all may learn, and all may be comforted.*
- *1 Corinthians 14:32 And the spirits of the prophets are subject to the prophets.*
- *1 Corinthians 14:33 For God is not the author of confusion, but of peace, as in all churches of the saints.*

Order is important. We should not fall over one another when operating in ministry for the Lord. There is no need to push and shove. Prophecy is the key to the Kingdom of

Heaven (Matthew 16:19). We cannot all put our key in the keyhole at the same time. This behavior will only serve to overwhelm the hearer. We should prophesy in a way that will be most beneficial for the hearer and not those that are operating in the gift. Though the Holy Spirit gives us the unction to prophesy, this does not mean that we are not responsible for how and when it comes out of our mouths. The spirits of the prophets are controlled by the people prophesying. Avoid acting as if you cannot control the urge to blurt out a prophetic Word. A strong urge from the Holy Ghost does not give anyone the right to take over the prophetic process. Leave room for respect, order and peace in ministry.

Verbal Confirmation

- *Luke 8:46 And Jesus said, Somebody hath touched Me: for I perceive that virtue is gone out of Me.*
- *Acts 3:6 Then Peter said, Silver and gold have I none; but such as I have, give I thee: In the Name of Jesus Christ of Nazareth, rise up and walk.*

To operate as a team, good verbal communication is needed. I have noticed in the Scriptures that people in the healing business often give verbal cues that the power of God is manifesting. In Acts 3:6, Peter says, "such as I have, give I thee." This is a verbal cue to John, his apostolic partner in ministry, the gift of healing is manifesting. Now, John knows that the Holy Ghost has chosen Peter to manifest this gift and he should look to play a support role. We do not see John jump in to lift the lame man up from the ground when he has not been given the anointing to do so. Clearly, John the apostle has the gift of healing and the ability to manifest it. However, Peter's verbal acknowledgment of the manifestation of the gift allow them to function decently and in order as a team.

Elders' Prayer of Faith

- *James 5:14 Is any sick among you? Let him call for the elders of the church; and let them pray over him, anointing him with oil in the Name of the Lord:*
- *James 5:15 And the prayer of faith shall save the sick, and the Lord shall raise him up; and if he have committed sins, they shall be forgiven him.*
- *James 5:16 Confess your faults one to another, and pray one for another, that ye may be healed. The effectual fervent prayer of a righteous man availeth much.*

(See Chapter 14: Administering the Prayer of Faith for Healing & Deliverance).

The Greater Gifts

- *1 Corinthians 12:28 And God hath set some in the Church, first apostles, secondarily prophets, thirdly teachers, after that miracles, then gifts of healings, helps, governments, diversities of tongues.*
- *1 Corinthians 12:31 But covet earnestly the best gifts: and yet shew I unto you a more excellent way.*

On a prophetic healing team, each person should begin praying in the Spirit to stir up the manifestation of the Holy Ghost (2 Timothy 1:6) and open the door to flow in the greater gifts. The gifts of prophecy, healing and miracles obviously make it easier to expedite the healing and deliverance process. However, only the Holy Spirit knows a person's real issues. Only He knows the many layers of deliverance and healing that need to take place in a person's life. It is imperative that you use the gifts of the Spirit as they are made available by the Holy Ghost. You should use them in the order He distributes them. If God gives you a prophetic Word while you are waiting for your hands to heat up for the gifts of healings, release the prophetic word first. It could be that the healing will take place when the prophetic word is heard by "the sick" person. Move as you are led by the Spirit of God.

Binding and Loosing

- *Matthew 18:18 Verily I say unto you, Whatsoever ye shall bind on earth shall be bound in heaven: and whatsoever ye shall loose on earth shall be loosed in heaven.*
- *Matthew 18:19 Again I say unto you, that if two of you shall agree on earth as touching any thing that they shall ask, it shall be done for them of My Father which is in heaven.*
- *Matthew 18:20 For where two or three are gathered together in my name, there am I in the midst of them.*

Binding and loosing are the acts of using the keys of the Kingdom of Heaven to lock and unlock the spiritual door to something, respectively. In Matthew 16:13-20, the thing being unlocked (or loosed) on earth and in heaven is the identity of Jesus of Nazareth. He is prophetically revealed by Peter to be Christ, the Son of the Living God. It is Peter that inadvertently used the key of revelation (called the gift of prophecy) to release this truth into the world. Binding and loosing, then, are the acts of using the revelation gifts of the Holy Spirit (*e.g.,* word of wisdom, word of knowledge, prophecy, *etc.*) to set something or someone free by the power of the Holy Ghost or to arrest or prohibit something or someone (*i.e.,* an unclean spirit or principality) by that same power. When we cast a demon out of a person with a word and command him not to return, we are primarily using the gift of discerning of spirits to bind the unclean spirit and prohibit him from further activity in a person's life (Mark 9:25).

When There are No Elders

Unfortunately, there is a shortage of true elders in the Church. It is very possible that you can be worshipping in a church environment, devoid of any ministers who are trained and equipped in healing and deliverance. The point of this chapter is not to cause a roadblock in the life of any person that needs healing or deliverance when they cannot find a suitable elder in the church. In this case, a person should just pray that God will reveal the necessary Believers (elder or not) that are willing to stand with them to believe for their healing. When identified, simply follow the instructions in this book, just as if the elders or ministers of God were present.

- Chapter 16 -
Preparing for Healing & Deliverance Ministry

*And straightway, He constrained His disciples to get into the ship, and to go to the other side before unto Bethsaida, **while He sent away the people. And when He had sent them away, He departed into a mountain to pray**. And when even was come, the ship was in the midst of the sea, and He alone on the land (Mark 6:45-47, emphasis added).*

*And when they had passed over, they came into the land of Gennesaret, and drew to the shore. And when they were come out of the ship, straightway they knew Him, and ran through that whole region round about, **and began to carry about in beds those that were sick, where they heard He was. And whithersoever He entered, into villages, or cities, or country, they laid the sick in the streets, and besought Him that they might touch if it were but the border of His garment: and as many as touched Him were made whole** (Mark 6:53-56, emphasis added).*

Healing takes preparation. Deliverance ministry requires preparation. Every Christian would love to lay hands on the sick and see them recover. Many ministers long to have nationally renowned healing ministries. We want to see God's people healed. We want others to see healing power working through our hands. As wonderful as that would be (assuming we would not do it in pride), the fact remains that it takes spiritual work and preparation to bring forth real healing and deliverance.

Jesus had a strong prayer life. His prayer life prepared Him for His healing and deliverance ministry. When Jesus was in the land of Gennesaret, again, we see Him healing every person that was brought to Him on a sick bed. Jesus' anointing was so great that He healed in every village, city or country He entered. He did not even lay hands on anyone in this story, they touched Him and were healed.

What I want every deliverance minister to see is that before healings took place and Jesus' fame spread throughout the land, He separated Himself to pray. Jesus removed Himself from the crowds and prayed. He even sent His leadership staff away, so He could have time to pray in the Spirit, hear from the Lord and be filled with the Holy Ghost. You cannot give what you do not possess. You cannot cure people of sickness and disease unless you have enough *dunamis* power built-up within you. You cannot cast out demons with a word, without being built-up on your most holy faith (Jude 20).

Jesus took the time to get recharged in the Holy Ghost. He made it a point to be filled with the Spirit. Without this activity, He would not have been able to heal and cast out demons effectively. It takes power to do this. Grandma was right, "Much prayer, much power; little prayer, little power; no prayer, no power!" Power is only released by a life that has spent time praying in the Holy Ghost and being saturated in the Word of God.

Here is another example:

And it came to pass in those days, **that He went out into a mountain to pray, and continued all night in prayer to God.** *(Luke 6:12, emphasis added)*

And He came down with them, and stood in the plain, and the company of His disciples, and a great multitude of people out of all Judaea and Jerusalem, and from the sea coast of Tyre and Sidon, which came to hear Him, **and to be healed of their diseases; And they that were vexed with unclean spirits: and they were healed. And the whole multitude sought to touch Him: for there went virtue out of Him, and healed them all.** *(Luke 6:17-19, emphasis added)*

Did you see what just happened there? Jesus prayed all night. We know that He prayed in the Holy Ghost. He spent time with the Father. He discovered the Father's will on earth as it is in heaven. Because of praying all night, Jesus was able to heal every person that had an unclean spirit and any disease. But let me say it again, Jesus prayed all night long! When was the last time you prayed all night long because you knew you needed to operate in healing and deliverance power the next day? This is what I am telling you! We need to take our prayer lives up a notch. For most of us, more than several notches.

As ministers, we often allow the cares of life and church work to prevent us from having power. The original disciples knew this as well:

And in those days, when the number of the disciples was multiplied, there arose a murmuring of the Grecians against the Hebrews, because their widows were neglected in the daily ministration. Then the twelve called the multitude of the disciples unto them, and said, **It is not reason that we should leave the Word of God, and serve tables.** *Wherefore, brethren, look ye out among you seven men of honest report, full of the Holy Ghost and wisdom, whom we may appoint over this business.* **But we will give ourselves continually to prayer, and to the ministry of the Word.** *(Acts 6:1-4, emphasis added)*

You've got to see this! Because they had Jesus' example, the early apostles knew they must give themselves **continually** to prayer. They had to pray all the time. And we're not even talking about continually giving ourselves to the Word of God, yet. We are very distracted as ministers of God today. (I couldn't even start thinking about praying today until I made sure our church bills were paid and took care of a leak coming from the ceiling).

Did I mention we need to be fasting, as well? Remember the demon that would not come out because the disciples had not prayed and fasted (Matthew 17:21, Mark 9:29). This is because they did not have enough *dunamis* power to get the demon out. They needed to have spent time praying and fasting to get that kind of power. They needed to have spent time praying and fasting to get rid of their own unbelief.

Praying in tongues, fasting and spending lots of time in the Word of God must be the hallmark of a healing and deliverance minister. It must be the standard of a healing and deliverance ministry. It must be the bread and butter of a healing and deliverance church. A healing church must have an Intercession Team that is assigned to pray and fast.

I believe a healing and deliverance minister should have a lifestyle of praying at least one hour per day. I believe this based on the words of Jesus:

And He cometh unto the disciples, and findeth them asleep, and saith unto Peter, What, could ye not watch with Me one hour? (Matthew 26:40)

I am not saying this to be legalistic. Of course, you can have power if you pray according to the will of God for five minutes. But I believe, according the Scriptures, we must spend significant amounts of time in the presence of the Lord to truly have power that matters. This was the example of Jesus Christ our King. This will cause a lifestyle change on the part of most of us that desire to please God by faith for healing and deliverance.

- Part 5 -
When Healing Stops

The Revelation of Healing

- Chapter 17 -
Demons, Nightmares, Ungodly Dreams & Maintaining Your Healing

I grew up in the horror movie era of the eighties and the early nighties. In that era we were enthralled with movies like *Friday the 13th*, *Nightmare on Elm Street* and *Halloween*. I watched every last never-ending sequel of those movies. Jason, Freddie Krueger and Michael Myers haunted my thoughts. I was fascinated with any movie that had an ax, chainsaw, blood, butcher knife, a masked villain and a pretty girl falling while running and screaming in the middle of a forest. Those movies filled a generation of kids like me with the spirit of fear. We were afraid of the dark, afraid to sleep with our closet doors open, afraid to sleep with them closed, and afraid to look under our beds at night. I hated being scared as a child, but for some reason I couldn't wait to see the next scary movie. They eventually came out with a movie called *Scary Movie* while I was in college, and I watched that too. I became weirdly addicted to being scared, but hated the side effect of fear that went with it. (Isn't that the very nature of sin?!)

Because of this, I was well acquainted with nightmares as a child. I would always have this reoccurring dream that a skeleton man was chasing me with an ax, trying to kill me. As nightmares go, I always woke up screaming right before he caught and killed me. This is one of the worst things a child can experience. No one wants to wake up out of their sleep in such fear. It's always interesting to see how long it takes to realize that a dream was not real and come back to reality. I am still fascinated that the mind can make something seem so real in the dream realm.

I watched a lot of TV as a kid (as you can see). One day I was watching a documentary about dreams and nightmares. In it, an expert psychologist on dreams began to reveal where nightmares originate and how to stop them from recurring. (Man, I wish we had YouTube back then, so I could still watch it today.) She explained that nightmares are just a representation of your inner fears that will not stop, until you stand up to that which you fear. She explained that you could stop scary figures from chasing you in your dreams with axes, knives, guns, *etc.*, by simply deciding during the dream to attack them back. She said it was possible, during your dream, to imagine that you had a gun or other weapon and simply fire back at the monster in your dreams. She promised if you were diligent to do this just once, that your nightmares would cease or greatly diminish.

One night, as a child, before going to bed, I decided to test this theory. And sure enough, I had another terrible dream with the skeleton man chasing me down the street with an ax. I was conscious enough during my dream to imagine that I had a gun in my hand and fired back at my assailant. To my surprise, he evaporated and disappeared! I woke up in victory and in some disbelief. That Doctor of

Psychology was right! And I have never had that nightmare again.

Understanding the Spiritual Dream Realm

The dream realm is a spiritual realm given to mankind by God to allow Him access to our thought life while we are sleeping. God designed mankind with this ability, so He could communicate with us while we are in a state of mind of true faith. Meaning, we are in a mindset while sleeping where we cannot actively interfere with the things God is trying to reveal to us. In our sleep, we are in the one place (in a 24-hour period) where God can speak to us without any intellectual resistance. Dreams were meant by God to be a component of the prophetic gift of the Holy Ghost. They allow us to know more perfectly the will of God for our lives if we are diligent to seek wisdom from Him about their meaning(s). God is able to encourage or warn us about things to come in our dreams. Consider the following:

*And He said, Hear now My words: If there be a **prophet** among you, I the LORD will make Myself known unto him in a **vision**, and will speak unto him in a **dream**. (Numbers 12:6, emphasis added)*

*For God speaketh once, yea twice, yet man perceiveth it not. In a **dream, in a vision of the night**, when deep sleep falleth upon men, in slumberings upon the bed; **then He openeth the ears of men, and sealeth their instruction**, (Job 33:14-16, emphasis added)*

*And it shall come to pass in the last days, saith God, I will pour out of My Spirit upon all flesh: and your sons and your daughters shall **prophesy**, and your young men shall see **visions**, and your old men shall **dream dreams**... (Acts 2:17, emphasis added)*

These Scriptures are amazing truths. God shows us that He is often speaking to us multiple times, but we are not paying attention. Because He loves us, He uses our dreams to get our attention and send us warnings.

Unfortunately, because our enemy the devil is also a spirit being, he can pervert the prophetic gift and enter our dreams using fear and the works of the flesh. This is the basis for nightmares and other evil kinds of dreams. This is also why we should avoid watching scary movies or anything that is designed to bring fear into our lives. We must manage our eye gate. We must learn to guard our heart (Proverbs 4:20-23).

When I was a teenager I begin to wonder if it were possible to commit a sin while dreaming. For example, if you have sex with someone that is not your spouse (a wet dream... try to stay mature, it's okay to laugh) while dreaming, is it a sin? I posed this question to a good minister friend of mine 25 years ago, now a pastor, Leroy Anthony. He immediately spoke these profound words (I wonder if he even remembers this conversation or still agrees with this statement). I'm paraphrasing:

> *"Yes! Absolutely! If the devil cannot get you to sin while you are awake, then he will try to get you to sin while you are asleep. The devil is a liar and would love to slip in the back door on a child of God and catch you with your guard down. What better way to do this then when you are asleep?"*

I have never forgotten what he said, for there was great revelation in His statement.

Dreams and Defeating Unclean Spirits

I have had many questionable dreams since I was a child. I am over 40 years young now. One major revelation that I have received from God about dreams (especially the ones I receive that are not from God) is that they are tightly attached to how well I am managing my thought life. I have had many nightmares since I was a child (though not the one about the skeleton ax murderer anymore). Most of these nightmares center on someone or some group of people trying to converge on me against my will, to harm me in some way.

I now know that these dreams are a manifestation of my fears and an attack of the enemy on my mind by unclean spirits while I am sleeping. Over the years, I have changed my weapon of choice against the enemy to a sword instead of a gun (my favorite weapon is a light saber, I'm a big Star Wars fan), but the result is the same. If I am attacked by the enemy in my dreams, I am quick to pull out my sword and fight back!

In my adult years of having dreams, an interesting phenomenon has occurred. Whenever I am having a dream where the enemy is getting ready to attack me, I will always take out my sword to return the favor. But, I have noticed now when I take out my sword that the enemy turns and runs! Yes, you read that correctly. The enemies in my dreams, if they see me take out my sword, will just turn and run. They high-tail it out of there because they know what is getting ready to happen – a beat down! This very interesting occurrence in my dreams has given me a great appreciation for the following Scripture:

Submit yourselves therefore to God. Resist the devil, and he will flee from you. (James 4:7)

What a coward! The devil only wants to contend with you when you operate in fear.

Maintaining Your Healing & Deliverance

Now, how does all of this connect to the subject of healing and deliverance? I'm glad you asked! Over the years, I have seen a consistent pattern in my life concerning my dreams (and you probably experience this as well, without realizing it). I have discovered, whenever I am beginning to defeat the enemy in some area of my life (*e.g.*, lust, diet, fear, anger, impatience, *etc.*), it will not be long before I have a dream in that same area. For example, if I am successfully keeping my eyes on the amazing woman God gave me – my wife – it will not be long before I have a dream with a beautiful woman in it. If I am successfully eating right and exercising, it will not be long before I have a dream about desserts and all the wrong foods I desire.

If I am successfully controlling my emotions and the words that come out of my mouth, it will not be long before I have a dream about an ignorant or irresponsible person (because the enemy knows these kinds of people rub me the wrong way). Whenever I have decided to repent and start a new righteous habit in my life, it is not long before I have a dream that gives me the opportunity to undo this decision.

Why is this important to maintaining your healing and deliverance? Well, in order to maintain your healing or deliverance, you need to know that you will need to guard your heart and mind in order to stay delivered. The enemy is a liar and he does not at all care about your well-being (John 10:10). He will attack you by any means necessary to get you into bondage, again. If you are going to stay delivered and healed, you need to take this information seriously. Let's look at the Scriptures:

And when the devil had ended all the temptation, **he departed from Him for a season.** *(Luke 4:13, emphasis added)*

When the unclean spirit is gone out of a man, he walketh through dry places, seeking rest, and findeth none. Then he saith, **I will return into my house from whence I came out;** *and when he is come, he findeth it empty, swept, and garnished. Then goeth he, and taketh with himself seven other spirits more wicked than himself, and they enter in and dwell there:* **and the last state of that man is worse than the first.** *Even so shall it be also unto this wicked generation. (Matthew 12:43-45, emphasis added)*

Then asked they him, What man is that which said unto thee, Take up thy bed, and walk? And he that was healed wist not who it was: for Jesus had conveyed Himself away, a multitude being in that place. Afterward, Jesus findeth him in the temple, and said unto him, Behold, thou art made whole: **sin no more, lest a worse thing come unto thee.** *(John 5:12-14, emphasis added)*

Please don't miss this revelation. Just because you have been healed or delivered does not mean that you will be automatically healed and delivered forever. The enemy would very much like to come back into your life and cause that sickness, disease or demonic oppression to return. He would like to see you worse than you were before you got healed.

Remember that the enemy works through our minds. He works through the access we give him through our thought lives, through our imaginations (2 Corinthians 10:3-6). He knows that our thoughts ultimately determine who we become (Proverbs 23:7). As we have learned, casting out the unclean spirits from our lives allows our mind to be free to also eliminate the sicknesses and diseases associated with that bondage. Bondage in the mind leads to stress, depression and anxiety, manifesting themselves in sickness and disease.

If we do not protect our thoughts, we open the door to the enemy's schemes. Righteous thoughts are the key to maintaining our deliverance. Entertaining one wicked thought from the enemy can open the door for an unclean spirit to return to your life, create a stronghold and cause your old sickness or disease to return. Fight to keep your healing and deliverance. We are wise to be mindful of the enemy's old tricks:

Lest Satan should get an advantage of us: for we are not ignorant of his devices. (2 Corinthians 2:11)

Guard Your Heart

The Scriptures are filled with wisdom on guarding your heart and mind. It is good to stay delivered. It is very possible to remain healed. Here are some of my favorite Scriptures to help you live a mentally pure life:

*Be careful for nothing; but in every thing by prayer and supplication with thanksgiving let your requests be made known unto God. **And the peace of God, which passeth all understanding, shall keep your hearts and minds through Christ Jesus.** Finally, brethren, whatsoever things are true, whatsoever things are honest, whatsoever things are just, whatsoever things are pure, whatsoever things are lovely, whatsoever things are of good report; if* *there be any virtue, and if there be any praise, **think on these things.** Those things, which ye have both learned, and received, and heard, and seen in me, do: and the God of peace shall be with you. (Philippians 4:6-9, emphasis added)*

*Blessed is the man that walketh not in the counsel of the ungodly, nor standeth in the way of sinners, nor sitteth in the seat of the scornful. But his delight is in the law of the LORD; **and in His law doth he meditate day and night.** And he shall be like a tree planted by the rivers of water, that bringeth forth his fruit in his season; his leaf also shall not wither; and whatsoever he doeth shall prosper. (Psalm 1:1-3, emphasis added)*

***Wherewithal shall a young man cleanse his way? by taking heed thereto according to Thy Word.** With my whole heart have I sought Thee: O let me not wander from Thy commandments. **Thy Word have I hid in mine heart,** that I might not sin against Thee. Blessed art Thou, O Lord: teach me Thy statutes. With my lips, have I declared all the judgments of Thy mouth. I have rejoiced in the way of Thy testimonies, as much as in all riches. **I will meditate in Thy precepts,** and have respect unto Thy ways. I will delight myself in Thy statutes: I will not forget Thy Word. (Psalm 119:9-16, emphasis added)*

*My son, keep thy father's commandment, and forsake not the law of thy mother: bind them continually upon thine heart, and tie them about thy neck. When thou goest, it shall lead thee; **when thou sleepest, it shall keep thee; and when thou awakest, it shall talk with thee**. (Proverbs 6:20-22, emphasis added)*

*My son, attend to my words; incline thine ear unto my sayings. Let them not depart from thine eyes; **keep them*** *in the midst of thine heart. For they are life unto those that find them, and health to all their flesh. **Keep thy heart with all diligence; for out of it are the issues of life.** (Proverbs 20:20-23, emphasis added)*

God's Word will keep us even when we are sleeping. He is able to keep us from falling (Jude 1:24). Thank You, Jesus! Amen to that!

- Chapter 18 -
Why do Healing & Deliverance Fail?
(And What to Do about It)

Unfortunately, I have been involved with many scenarios where healing and deliverance has not worked. I have also been involved in scenarios where healing and deliverance has worked slowly, over a long period of time. I have attended and performed funerals in cases where we have prayed for a loved one to be healed and they still went home to be with the Lord. No matter the case, the result is that all these cases have caused me to know that there is still much work to do in my life and in the lives of God's people to cause His Kingdom to come and His will to be done on earth as it is in heaven.

If asked, I would be the first person to admit that I do not know everything about healing and deliverance. However, by stepping out on the faith the Lord has given me and refusing to quit until I see everything come to pass that God has revealed to me through His Word, I have learned much about the operation of the Holy Ghost and His desire to heal, set free and deliver.

This chapter reflects those things I have learned through the Word of God, my own experience in healing and the answers I have received from the Lord in prayer and meditation when healing has not manifested.

I would also like to counsel you not to get too concerned about why healing and deliverance sometimes fails. I have discovered that if we focus on believing in Jesus Christ and His Word, God will work miraculously more often than not. Remember, the issue with healing and deliverance is a problem for us to solve. The problem is not on God's side of the equation. He has finished His part of the work. We are still here on this planet so that we can discover His finished work and manifest it through our lives by faith.

Because I could write a book about each one of these, I am only committed to write a short comment concerning my thoughts on each one of these subjects. I hope they are helpful to you in your journey. Here are some of the reasons I believe healing and deliverance fails to occur (and what I believe we should do about it):

1) Because of Our Unbelief

*And when they were come to the multitude, there came to Him a certain man, kneeling down to Him, and saying, Lord, have mercy on my son: for he is lunatick, and sore vexed: for ofttimes he falleth into the fire, and oft into the water. And I brought him to Thy disciples, and they could not cure him. Then Jesus answered and said, O faithless and perverse generation, how long shall I be with you? How long shall I suffer you? Bring him hither to Me. And Jesus rebuked the devil; and he departed out of him: and the child was cured from that very hour. **Then came the disciples to Jesus apart, and said, Why could not we cast him out? And Jesus said unto them, Because of your unbelief:** for verily I say unto you, If ye have faith as a grain of mustard seed, ye shall say unto this mountain,*

Remove hence to yonder place; and it shall remove; and nothing shall be impossible unto you. **Howbeit this kind goeth not out but by prayer and fasting.** *(Matthew 17:14-21, emphasis added)*

This is one of the most controversial reasons why healing and deliverance is sometimes unsuccessful. It is especially hard to swallow when we lose a loved one in the process. The reason this is difficult to swallow is because it places the reason for failure squarely back in our court. Jesus was clear to His disciples, and I imagine He looked them square in the eyes when He said, "Because of your unbelief!"

Quite honestly, sometimes we just do not have enough faith power to get a demon to come out. Sometimes we do not have enough anointing (though we would like to think we do) to bring a healing to pass. Obviously, it has nothing to do with God's will to heal the person. He is willing to heal. He gave His Son, Jesus Christ, specifically to die for our healing. In this Scripture, had Jesus not showed up, someone would have said, "It must not be God's will to heal your boy!" However, Jesus did arrive despite the disciples' failure and demonstrated that it was still the will of the Father to heal.

What was the solution? In this scenario, Jesus tells the disciples that fasting and prayer were required. I believe that Jesus is teaching the disciples that fasting and prayer will eliminate their unbelief, so they can use their most holy faith (unhindered by doubt and fear) to be successful in the future. The solution: we need to improve our prayer and fasting lives, so we can be ready to carry more of the anointing of God to heal when the need arises.

2) The Lack of Teaching

And He went out from thence, and came into His own country; and His disciples follow Him. And when the sabbath day was come, He began to teach in the synagogue: and many hearing Him were astonished, saying, From whence hath this Man these things? And what wisdom is this which is given unto Him, that even such mighty works are wrought by His hands? Is not this the carpenter, the son of Mary, the brother of James, and Joses, and of Juda, and Simon? And are not His sisters here with us? And they were offended at Him. But Jesus said unto them, A prophet is not without honour, but in his own country, and among his own kin, and in his own house. **And He could there do no mighty work,** *save that He laid His hands upon a few sick folk, and healed them.* **And He marvelled because of their unbelief. And He went round about the villages, teaching.** *(Mark 6:1-6, emphasis added)*

This is a unique scenario of unbelief. In this case, there was so much unbelief that not even Jesus, the Master Healer, could do any mighty works. Imagine that, even Jesus could not operate in healing at times.

Notice, however, that Jesus does not go around proclaiming that God is no longer in the healing business or that it was not the Father's will to bring forth healing in Nazareth. Nope, Jesus knew the solution to cause more healings to come to pass. He knew that sometimes healing will not flow freely, unless the ground of God's people's hearts is softened and made fertile through the ministry of teaching. Specifically, we know that Jesus taught and then preached the Gospel of the Kingdom, opening the door afterwards for healing (Matthew 4:23). Teaching opens the door for healing.

The solution: we need to teach more about healing and deliverance. This is a book of teaching. It shall be distributed throughout the land to bless God's people. This book will open the door wider for our generation to be healed, set free and delivered. We must start more churches where we believe and disciple the saints to heal and deliver. We need to start more training centers. We need to teach people how to cast out demons. We need to teach the saints how to flow in the ministry of laying on of hands, responsibly.

3) The Restitution of All Things

*Repent ye therefore, and be converted, that your sins may be blotted out, **when the times of refreshing shall come from the presence of the Lord**; And He shall send Jesus Christ, which before was preached unto you: Whom the heaven must receive **until the times of restitution of all things**, which God hath spoken by the mouth of all His holy prophets since the world began. (Acts 3:19-21, emphasis added)*

Sometimes, there is not enough anointing available in the Body of Christ to operate in the gifts of the Holy Ghost in a season or generation. Sometimes, the grace of God to do something is just not available. Jesus, the head of the Church, controls how much of His grace is available to operate in the power of His gifts.

For example, the Protestant Reformation was started in the early 1500s by Martin Luther. The Lutheran denomination was started to harness the anointing of this time of restitution that came from the presence of the Lord. This does not mean that no one could be saved by grace through faith until Martin Luther arrived. It only means that it was very difficult for God's people to accept Jesus Christ before that period because the revelation needed (through teaching) was not widely available. Similarly, the power of the Holy Ghost to speak in tongues was restored to the Church again in 1905 during the Azusa Street revival. The ability to speak in tongues existed before 1905, but the ability for the Church to operate in it in mass quantities did not flow again until 1905. This started the Pentecostal Reformation almost 1,900 years after Jesus released it on the day of Pentecost, back in Acts chapter 2. The Church of God in Christ (COGIC), Assemblies of God, Church of God and other denominations were started by Christ to harness this time of restitution and bring order to the movement.

The solution: whenever it is difficult to flow in the gifts or graces of the Holy Ghost, it may be that we need a time of refreshing to come from the Lord to flow in it more freely in our generation. The job of the Church during this time is to teach sound Bible principles and pray that Jesus will refresh us to receive more. We cannot wait until the manifestation comes before we start teaching about it. We must be brave to uphold the Word of God, even if we do not yet know how to operate in it. The manifestation will come later, as it has throughout Church history.

What we should not do is begin teaching that certain gifts and graces are no longer available to the Body of Christ whenever we are not seeing them manifest as quickly as we would like. We do not know why Jesus causes certain graces and gifts to be limited in certain seasons. That is not our concern (Acts 1:7). Our job is to preach the truth, ask God for more of His glory and operate in the revelation we have been given to the best of our ability.

4) The Spirit of Religion and Tradition

Making the Word of God of none effect through your tradition, which ye have delivered: and many such like things do ye. (Mark 7:13)

Having a form of godliness, but denying the power thereof: from such turn away. (2 Timothy 3:5)

Unfortunately, we are very often more dedicated to what our denominations or specific churches teach more than we care about the Word of God. Upon much study of the Word and observation of "church folks," I have concluded that too many people who attend church services do not really believe in Jesus Christ. Many of God's people attend church meetings for social reasons rather than to seek the face of Jesus. For this reason, we get very upset when someone attempts to operate according to the Scriptures, whenever that activity is outside of the norm of our traditions.

There are too many of us in the Church that say we believe in Jesus Christ but are not willing to do the things He did. Jesus healed the sick, raised the dead, worked miracles, laid hands, prayed in the Spirit, cast out demons, sacrificed His life for others, cared for the poor and preached the gospel of the Kingdom.

The solution: we should follow the example of Christ. Anything else is done in the spirit of the Pharisees.

5) Generational Curses

Thou shalt have no other gods before Me. Thou shalt not make unto thee any graven image, or any likeness of any thing that is in heaven above, or that is in the earth beneath, or that is in the water under the earth: thou shalt not bow down thyself to them, nor serve them: for I the LORD thy God am a jealous God, visiting the iniquity of the fathers upon the children unto the third and fourth generation of them that hate me... (Exodus 20:3-5)

Let Thine ear now be attentive, and Thine eyes open, that Thou mayest hear the prayer of Thy servant, which I pray before Thee now, day and night, for the children of Israel, Thy servants, and confess the sins of the children of Israel, which we have sinned against Thee: both I and my father's house have sinned. (Nehemiah 1:6)

And the seed of Israel separated themselves from all strangers, and stood and confessed their sins, and the iniquities of their fathers. (Nehemiah 9:2)

It is not uncommon to be in a deliverance session with someone that seems to be going nowhere (and taking forever) when the Holy Spirit reveals that one of their ancestors has made a vow to Satan, knowingly or unknowingly. This kind of vow making usually takes the form of their ancestor (*e.g.*, a grandfather, grandmother, *etc.*) being in a fraternal organization like the Masons or Eastern Stars, where they had to swear a vow of secrecy as a natural part of progressing through the ranks. Because this is modern day idol worship, participating in these kinds of things gives the devil a foothold in a person's life and in the lives of their children and children's children, creating a generational curse.

The solution: when this occurs, we are usually led to have the person in the deliverance chair renounce the specific sin of their family as it is revealed to us and start all over again with the deliverance session (exhausted).

6) Unforgiveness

Therefore is the kingdom of heaven likened unto a certain king, which would take account of his servants. And when he had begun to reckon, one was brought unto him, which owed him ten thousand talents. But forasmuch as he had not to pay, his lord commanded him to be sold, and his wife, and children, and all that he had, and payment to be made. The servant therefore fell down, and worshipped him, saying, Lord, have patience with me, and I will pay thee all. Then, the lord of that servant was moved with compassion, and loosed him, and forgave him the debt. But the same servant went out, and found one of his fellowservants, which owed him an hundred pence: and he laid hands on him, and took him by the throat, saying, Pay me that thou owest. And his fellowservant fell down at his feet, and besought him, saying, Have patience with me, and I will pay thee all. And he would not: but went and cast him into prison, till he should pay the debt. So, when his fellowservants saw what was done, they were very sorry, and came and told unto their lord all that was done. Then, his lord, after that he had called him, said unto him, O thou wicked servant, I forgave thee all that debt, because thou desiredst me: Shouldest not thou also have had compassion on thy fellowservant, even as I had pity on thee? **And his lord was wroth, and delivered him to the tormentors, till he should pay all that was due unto him. So likewise shall My Heavenly Father do also unto you, if ye from your hearts forgive not every one his brother their trespasses.** *(Matthew 18:23-35, emphasis added)*

In my experience, the number one reason that a person cannot get delivered is because they are harboring unforgiveness toward someone. It is usually a close relative or a spouse. I have found unforgiveness inside a person to be a hotbed for demonic activity that leads to stress and anxiety. This kind of stress and anxiety leads to hair loss, unhealthy weight loss, high blood pressure, depression, unexplained tumors and even cancer. Stress is the number one reason, that I have seen, that leads to a myriad of unexplained manifestations of sickness and disease. This occurs because the person is being tormented by unclean spirits. It is always amazing to see a person's entire countenance improve overnight, when we simply get them to forgive.

The solution: lead the person in a prayer of forgiveness towards their family member (or whoever has offended them) and even get them to personally and verbally forgive that person if necessary.

7) The Cares of this World

He also that received seed among the thorns is he that heareth the Word; and the care of this world, and the deceitfulness of riches, choke the word, and he becometh unfruitful. (Matthew 13:22)

But we will give ourselves continually to prayer, and to the ministry of the Word. (Acts 6:4)

Because I am a pastor, I get the unique opportunity to study God's people every week. I get the opportunity to observe the state of God's flock to see what drives and motivates the sheep to worship the Father (or not). One thing that I have noticed as a hindrance to Christ's Church is its 24-hour access to the world. Because we live in the technology age, we are constantly bombarded with information through TV, Facebook, Twitter, Instagram, email from our jobs, cellphone updates and notifications, *etc.* There are so many things in which we obligate ourselves to participate, like soccer league for our kids and the next ballet or piano recital. We are more engrossed in the cares of this world than ever before, and it leaves little time to sit down with our Bibles to pray and seek the face of the Father in heaven. I have found that truly pursuing the will of Jesus Christ is a very low priority for most Christians.

Consequently, most members want to attend a seeker-sensitive church with a non-authoritative environment, where they can sit in the back, hear some good music, get a feel-good sermon and go back home, while someone else attends to the Lord's business. We just do not have any real time for Jesus.

The problem with all of this is that it takes time to truly cultivate a faith-rich environment, where we can truly experience a move of God. The early disciples knew this and appointed others in the Church that would tend to the cares of this world among God's people, while they spent time in the Word and prayer. This occurred to make sure they had direct access to the supernatural power of the Holy Ghost.

As a local church pastor, it is very difficult at times to get God's people focused long enough to charge the atmosphere with enough faith, devoid of unbelief, to truly experience God's glory for our lives. Sometimes, we do not have the attention span, desire, motivation or faith necessary to contact the Father once or twice a week in the assembly of the saints. After a 2-hour church service, most people are ready to go home, even if one more hour would change their lives forever.

One of the largest reasons for this is because most people have not even looked at their Bibles since the last time they were in a meeting. And it is very difficult to get most of God's people to study their Bibles and pray in their homes. I can always hear the inner groans of conviction within the saints whenever I start preaching and teaching about their responsibility to upgrade their relationship with Jesus in their private time. It is hard to get God's people to prioritize the Kingdom of God in their lives.

8) Seek First the Kingdom

But seek ye first the Kingdom of God, and His righteousness; and all these things shall be added unto you. (Matthew 6:33)

We are commanded to seek God's Kingdom and His way of being correct, first. That means we should pray before seeking the aspirin bottle. This means we should fast before going to the doctor. This means we should lay prostrate on the altar before disconnecting a loved one from life support. We are to seek God's Kingdom – first!

However, after we have prayed, fasted, cried, petitioned the courts of heaven, followed godly counsel, sat in sackcloth and ashes, and there is still no healing or deliverance on the horizon, it is time to seek a "second" option. If we have sought the Kingdom first and there is no relief, then I see no reason why we cannot seek wise counsel from doctors, psychologists and any other healthcare professionals to undergo surgery, receive medication or any other healthcare solution until the Lord shows us otherwise.

The solution: our God is a merciful God and He is well able to instruct us to make a hospital visit by the voice of His Word, just as well as send us to a church service to be healed. Unfortunately, too many of us are programed to reach into the medicine cabinet before seeking the Lord for healing and deliverance by His Spirit. By doing this, we unknowingly forfeit our true healing and breakthrough from the Lord. We must increase our faith in Jesus.

9) Forgiveness of Sins

And, behold, they brought to Him a man sick of the palsy, lying on a bed: and Jesus seeing their faith said unto the sick of the palsy; Son, be of good cheer; thy sins be forgiven thee. (Matthew 9:2)

Then said Jesus to them again, Peace be unto you: as My Father hath sent Me, even so send I you. And when He had said this, He breathed on them, and saith unto them, Receive ye the Holy Ghost: Whose soever sins ye remit, they are remitted unto them; and whose soever sins ye retain, they are retained. (John 20:21-23)

Often, because we are Holy Ghost filled, fire baptized Believers in Jesus Christ, we are anxious to supernaturally thrust the powers of heaven on any lost soul we can find. Because we know the resources of the Lord are extremely abundant, we are grieved whenever we see one lamb of God walking around without every ounce of prosperity that Jesus gave His life securing. This causes us to be very heavy handed to press everyone we know to be healed and totally delivered.

Sometimes, however, people are too weary to receive physical healing or to be released from demonic oppression. Sometimes, a person has spent a lifetime battling with their own vices, sins, addictions, tragedies and misfortunes. At the final hour on a sick bed, a person may be tired of battling in this life and they just want to go home to be with the Lord. The only thing that is hindering a person from taking a deep breath and going home to be with Jesus is that they are so tormented by their past sins and missed opportunities with their loved ones, they cannot get their souls to enter His rest peacefully. At this time, we have the authority – those of us that are mature – to simply say, "Be at peace, it is okay, your sins are forgiven."

This is often the last thing a person's loved ones want to hear. Sometimes, family members want to keep a sick loved one here because they have not properly prepared themselves independently of their influence and resources. They are not ready to live life on their own two feet. Some relatives want a wayward family member to suffer for the wrong they have done until their final breath. We do not always know why some have lived wayward lives or why they have taken the path of wickedness or made poor decisions. We each have our own journey and it is not up to us to judge what it will take for a person to finally see that Jesus Christ is King of kings and Lord of lords. Even the thief on the cross was given mercy. Perhaps your mercy upon a lost soul in the final hour will be the seed and water that will sprout up into everlasting life.

The solution: tell the person their sins are forgiven. Ask them if they desire prayer. Offer the free gift of Jesus Christ as their Lord and personal Savior if they are willing to receive it.

10) Dealing with Death

For whether we live, we live unto the Lord; and whether we die, we die unto the Lord: whether we live therefore, or die, we are the Lord's. (Romans 14:8)

But I would not have you to be ignorant, brethren, concerning them which are asleep, that ye sorrow not, even as others which have no hope. For if we believe that Jesus died and rose again, even so them also which sleep in Jesus will God bring with Him. (1 Thessalonians 4:13-14)

We will see our loved ones again if they have accepted Jesus Christ as Lord. If not, we must face the reality that they lived life as they saw fit and that is their prerogative, not ours. At the end of the day we all belong to God, whether saved or unsaved.

None of us will live as long or as prosperous as we would like in this life. That is the purpose of eternity. In light of this, we should take every moment to cherish those we love and take every opportunity to celebrate them while they are alive.

The solution: when a person is grieving because they have lost a loved one, especially after believing for their healing, give them space to grieve in their own way. Talk less and listen more. Sometimes, it is best to just sit with the bereaved and say nothing at all. Some wounds only heal with time. We will not be made perfect until we receive our resurrected bodies and see the Lord, the everlasting King, face to face.

Do not spend inordinate amounts of time trying to explain to someone in pain why healing did not work for their loved one. They will not be able to process your explanation anyway. Assure them that you will be there for them and deliver on that promise as much as it depends on you. The Lord willing, you may be all the Jesus they needed if you walk in unconditional love.

11) Lack of Authority

But when Jesus heard it, He answered him, saying, Fear not: believe only, and she shall be made whole. And when He came into the house, He suffered no man to go in, save

Peter, and James, and John, **and the father and the mother of the maiden.** *(Luke 8:50-51, emphasis added)*

If you study the healing ministry of Jesus closely, you will see that He never steps over those that have God-given authority over the sick (*e.g.,* parents, guardians, masters, *etc.*). This is especially true in the case of children. Jesus never goes beyond what the parents have asked of Him. Jesus never moves forward without the cooperation of the person in charge of the sick, diseased or demon possessed. This is important to remember, because God is a God of inherent authority and order.

I have been in many hospital rooms where a person needs to be healed, but the family member that has authority over this sick person is unwilling to allow anyone to pray over them. I have literally seen a young man dying and his father did not want any of us "healing folk" around his son. In these scenarios, if you attempt to pray and lay hands anyway, I have seen that the power of God will not manifest. At the very least, it will be very weak.

It is important to honor those who oversee the sick. They have the final say on whether that person will have access to healing. This can be hard when dealing with a close friend.

The solution: respect the family's wishes and pray that God will cause them to give you an open door to bring healing.

12) Failure to Remove Unbelievers

*And all wept, and bewailed her: but He said, Weep not; she is not dead, but sleepeth. And they laughed Him to scorn, knowing that she was dead. **And He put them all out**, and took her by the hand, and called, saying, Maid, arise.*

And her spirit came again, and she arose straightway: and He commanded to give her meat. (Luke 8:52-55, emphasis added)

The worst kinds of people to have around when praying for healing are what I call "unbelieving Believers." These are Christians that do not believe in healing or the gifts of the Holy Ghost (especially the gift of speaking in tongues). These kinds of Christians will almost always stop a healing from taking place. They are filled with the spirit of religion.

The solution: Jesus did not tolerate these kinds of religious people when trying to manifest the power of God. He knew their unbelief would suck all the power out of the healing room. He knew it was imperative to remove as much unbelief as possible from the healing exercise.

I have been careful to make sure I am not walking in fear, unbelief or doubt when in the healing room. I will not hesitate to remove myself from the healing room if I am fatigued and beginning to operate with a low expectation for healing. Healing requires faith in the supernatural power of God. There is no unbelief allowed.

13) Pride

But He giveth more grace. Wherefore He saith, God resisteth the proud, but giveth grace unto the humble. Submit yourselves therefore to God. Resist the devil, and he will flee from you. (James 4:6-7)

Likewise, ye younger, submit yourselves unto the elder. Yea, all of you be subject one to another, and be clothed with humility: for God resisteth the proud, and giveth grace to the humble. Humble yourselves therefore under the mighty Hand of God, that He may exalt you in due time... (1 Peter 5:5-6)

Some people want to walk in the power of healing and deliverance for all the wrong reasons. Their true desire is that others will think of them as extra anointed. They want to prove to others that the way they see the Scriptures is "the" correct way. They see healing and deliverance as a means to force what they believe on others. They are concerned with building their own kingdom and not God's Kingdom. They are overwhelmed with trying to bring their own agenda to pass.

This kind of person is filled with pride. Pride wants all the glory without making the sacrifices necessary to walk in the power of God, without taking any shortcuts. God will never allow His true power to be given to anyone with this mindset.

The solution: the Word says that God resists the proud. Proud people have a problem submitting to authority. Submitting to God's ordained authorities is necessary to truly flow in the power and anointing of the Holy Ghost. Submit to the authorities that God has placed in your life.

The Restitution of Healing & Deliverance

It is my heart's desire that healing and deliverance be fully restored to the Church in this generation. It has been the heart's desire of many before me. I would like to see the fulness of the things for which our King, Jesus Christ, died manifest in this generation. I believe this is necessary to bring about the restitution of all things. I believe Jesus is waiting for His bride, the Church, to mature into a grown Proverbs 31 woman, able to completely make the enemies of Christ His footstool. I believe the Church is still being trained and equipped to rule at the tops of the mountains of this world.

I am still hopeful that God's people have a desire to advance the Kingdom of God on earth as it is in heaven. I believe that is your desire because you have read this book. I believe this book will change a generation into Mark 16:17-18 disciples. I release my faith that this revelation of healing will travel to the ends of the earth.

I pray that God will release a mantle of healing and deliverance upon your life like never before. I decree you will walk in the anointed gifts of healing and discerning of spirits. I pray you will manifest them in faith, hope and charity (1 Corinthians 13:13). I release the anointing of this book upon your life in the same Spirit of power, love and a sound mind, as it was written (2 Timothy 1:7).

Beloved, I wish above all things that you may prosper and be in health, even as your soul prospers (3 John 1:2)!

In Jesus' Name!

Another Great Kingdom Resource by Larry Henderson, Jr.

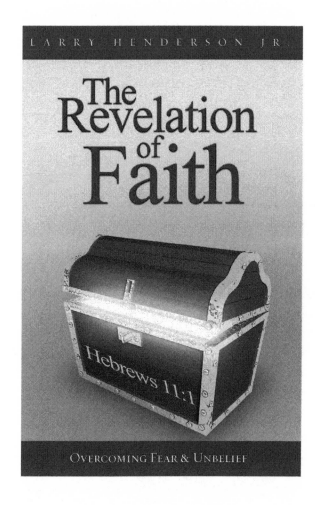

Order on Amazon!

Made in the USA
Columbia, SC
09 September 2018